Lecture Notes
in Business Information Processing

506

LNBIP reports state-of-the-art results in areas related to business information systems and industrial application software development – timely, at a high level, and in both printed and electronic form.

The type of material published includes

- Proceedings (published in time for the respective event)
- Postproceedings (consisting of thoroughly revised and/or extended final papers)
- Other edited monographs (such as, for example, project reports or invited volumes)
- Tutorials (coherently integrated collections of lectures given at advanced courses, seminars, schools, etc.)
- Award-winning or exceptional theses

LNBIP is abstracted/indexed in DBLP, EI and Scopus. LNBIP volumes are also submitted for the inclusion in ISI Proceedings.

Sérgio Pedro Duarte · António Lobo ·
Boris Delibašić · Daouda Kamissoko
Editors

Decision Support Systems XIV

Human-Centric Group Decision, Negotiation and Decision Support Systems for Societal Transitions

10th International Conference on Decision
Support System Technology, ICDSST 2024
Porto, Portugal, June 3–5, 2024
Proceedings

 Springer

Editors
Sérgio Pedro Duarte
University of Porto
Porto, Portugal

António Lobo
University of Porto
Porto, Portugal

Boris Delibašić
University of Belgrade
Belgrade, Serbia

Daouda Kamissoko
IMT Mines Albi
Albi, France

ISSN 1865-1348 ISSN 1865-1356 (electronic)
Lecture Notes in Business Information Processing
ISBN 978-3-031-59375-8 ISBN 978-3-031-59376-5 (eBook)
https://doi.org/10.1007/978-3-031-59376-5

This Springer imprint is published by the registered company Springer Nature Switzerland AG
The registered company address is: Gewerbestrasse 11, 6330 Cham, Switzerland

Paper in this product is recyclable.

Preface

This fourteenth edition of the EWG-DSS Decision Support Systems published in the LNBIP series presents a selection of high-quality papers from the 10th International Conference on Decision Support System Technology (ICDSST 2024), held in Porto, Portugal, from 3–5 June, 2024. The conference was held in parallel with the 24th International Conference on Group Decision and Negotiation. Both conferences were under the main theme "Human-centric decision and negotiation support for societal transitions". The event was organized by a local team from the Faculty of Engineering of the University of Porto, in collaboration with both the EURO Working Group on Decision Support Systems (EWG-DSS) and the Group Decision and Negotiation section from INFORMS.

This joint conference happened ten years after the last conference the two groups collaborated to organize, which was held in Toulouse, France, with a special focus: Group Decision Making and Web 3.0. That year marked the beginning of the ICDSST conferences, officially starting the next year in Belgrade. The EWG-DSS series of International Conferences on Decision Support System Technology (ICDSST) was planned to consolidate the tradition of annual events organized by the EWG-DSS in offering a platform for European and international DSS communities, comprising the academic and industrial sectors, to present state-of-the-art DSS research and developments, to discuss current challenges that surround decision-making processes, to exchange ideas about realistic and innovative solutions, and to co-develop potential business opportunities.

Human-Centric Decision and Negotiation Support for Societal Transitions

The topic selected for the event reflected the interests of both groups and, as usual, the current world scene and research trends.

In a time when technology is rapidly evolving, decision-makers face two major challenges: (1) using technology to improve the decision process, and (2) ensuring that decisions really support the best interests of the actors involved. On the one hand, the evolution of machine learning and AI offers incredible benefits; on the other hand, we as technology creators must ensure that humans remain the main beneficiaries of new services, software, and policies.

The transition period society is going through has brought even more complexity to decision processes, by increasing uncertainty regarding the future. Whatever is our research focus (climate, energy, AI, automation, information and communication technology, etc.), change, transition, and challenges are recurrent. Add uncertainty to the mix and we have highly complex decision processes, with several interested actors and multiple levels of goals. This recurring uncertainty has impacts on economics, employment, demographics, politics, and other societal concerns.

Accordingly, the topics promoted discussions on the human and technological aspects of decision-making processes to build bridges between the two domains:

1. Technology as a support tool: from the technological perspective, research must demonstrate that technology can be trusted and that proposed solutions are safe, inclusive, and fair.
2. From the human perspective, research should ensure that humans remain at the center of the decisions, with participatory and negotiation processes that promote co-creation and co-design of technology, services, and regulations. Such reliable decision processes increase trust in and fairness of the decisions.

These two perspectives were brought to the conference from the experience that each group has in the decision-making domain.

This EWG-DSS LNBIP Springer edition includes contributions selected via a single-blind evaluation process. Each selected paper was reviewed by at least three experts from the Program Committee. The review process of one contribution from two of the guest editors was handled by other Program Committee members. Through rigorous review and revision, 10 out of 29 submissions were selected for publication in this 14th EWG-DSS Springer LNBIP Edition. The selected papers are representative of the current and recent DSS research and application advancements.

Technology As a Support Tool

The volume here presented is a collection of the best papers submitted to the topic "Technology as support tool" and is organized in two sections.

(1) Decision support tools and methods

   The first section presents six papers dedicated to studying decision processes supported by modern technologies. By taking advantage of data mining, machine learning, neural networks, process mining, multi-criteria decision analysis, and simulation techniques, the authors propose new approaches, frameworks, and tools adapted to the complex multi-level systems which have evolved in industry.

(2) Decision factors and behaviors

   This section comprises four papers focused on analyzing the experience and perception users have when using DSS and other digital tools and how they are influenced by their experience. The papers include behavioral studies aiming at understanding how decision-makers make decisions, a user experience examination of AI-based tools in the health context, and a framework to assess consumers' perceptions in the food industry. A final paper is dedicated to exploring the knowledge transfer capabilities of digital tools.

We would like to thank many people who greatly helped the success of this LNBIP book. First of all, we would like to thank Springer for giving us the opportunity to guest edit the DSS book, and we especially wish to express our sincere gratitude to the Springer staff, who provided us with timely professional guidance and advice during the volume editing process. Secondly, we need to thank all the authors for submitting their state-of-the-art work to be considered for this LNBIP volume. Thirdly, we wish to express our gratitude to all the reviewers who volunteered to help with the selection and improvement of the papers.

We believe that this EWG-DSS Springer LNBIP volume has selected a collection of high-quality and interesting research papers addressing the conference's main theme and related topics. We hope the readers will enjoy the publication!

March 2024

Sérgio Pedro Duarte\
António Lobo\
Boris Delibašić\
Daouda Kamissoko

Organization

Conference Chairs

Sérgio Pedro Duarte   University of Porto, Portugal
Pascale Zaraté   University Toulouse Capitole - IRIT, France

Program Committee Chairs

António Lobo   University of Porto, Portugal
Boris Delibašić   University of Belgrade, Serbia
Tomasz Wachowicz   University of Economics in Katowice, Poland

Organizing Committee

Carlos Rodrigues   University of Porto, Portugal
Marta Campos Ferreira   INESC TEC, University of Porto, Portugal
Sara Ferreira   University of Porto, Portugal

Program Committee

Abdelkader Adla   University of Oran, Algeria
Ana Paula Costa   Federal University of Pernambuco, Brazil
Antonio de Nicola   ENEA, Italy
Carolina Lino Martins   UFPE/UFMS, Brazil
Danielle Costa Morais   Federal University of Pernambuco, Brazil
Daouda Kamissoko   IMT Mines - Albi, France
Ewa Roszkowska   Bialystok University of Technology, Poland
François Pinet   INRAE, France
Fuad Aleskerov   HSE, Russia
Gert-Jan de Vreede   University of South Florida, USA
Haiyan Xu   Nanjing University of Aeronautics and Astronautics, China

Hannu Nurmi   University of Turku, Finland
Jason Papathanasiou   University of Macedonia, Greece
Jorge Freire de Sousa   University of Porto, Portugal

José Moreno-Jiménez	Universidad de Zaragoza, Spain
José Pedro Tavares	University of Porto, Portugal
Konstantinos Vergidis	University of Macedonia, Greece
Liping Fang	Toronto Metropolitan University, Canada
Luís Dias	University of Coimbra, Portugal
Mareike Schoop	University of Hohenheim, Germany
María Teresa Escobar	Universidad de Zaragoza, Spain
Marta Campos Ferreira	University of Porto, Portugal
Masahide Horita	University of Tokyo, Japan
Michael Filzmoser	Vienna University of Technology, Austria
Muhammed-Fatih Kaya	University of Hohenheim, Germany
Nannan Wu	Nanjing University of Inf. Science and Technology, China
Pavlos Delias	International Hellenic University, Greece
Przemysław Szufel	Warsaw School of Economics, Poland
Rosaldo Rossetti	University of Porto, Portugal
Rudolf Vetschera	University of Vienna, Austria
Sandro Radovanović	University of Belgrade, Serbia
Sara Ferreira	University of Porto, Portugal
Sean Eom	Southeast Missouri State University, USA
Shawei He	Nanjing University of Aeronautics and Astronautics, China
Teresa Galvão	University of Porto, Portugal
Thiago Sobral	University of Porto, Portugal
Tomasz Szapiro	Warsaw School of Economics, Poland
Tung X. Bui	University of Hawaii, USA

Contents

Decision Support Tools and Methods

Understanding Supply Chain Resilience as a Multi-level Framework: A Systematic Literature Review

Guoqing Zhao[1], Guoyu Zhao[2]([✉]), Nasiru Zubairu[3], Xiaoning Chen[4], Femi Olan[5], Denis Dennehy[1], and Paul Jones[1]

[1] School of Management, Swansea University, Swansea, UK
{guoqing.zhao,denis.dennehy,w.p.jones}@swansea.ac.uk
[2] School of Management, Henan University of Technology, Zhengzhou, China
1299095006@qq.com
[3] Faculty of Transport and Logistics, Muscat University, Muscat, Oman
nzubariu@muscatuniversity.edu.om
[4] Plymouth Business School, University of Plymouth, Plymouth, UK
xiaoning.chen@plymouth.ac.uk
[5] Essex Business School, University of Essex, Colchester, UK
femi.olan@essex.ac.uk

Abstract. Supply chain resilience (SCRes) has received considerable attention from scholars and practitioners because organizations and supply chains are facing increasing disasters, uncertainties, and risks. They seek to survive disruptions and return to their original or a better state, and thereby achieve competitive advantage. However, existing studies investigate SCRes mainly from organizational and supply chain perspectives, which limits scholars' and practitioners' understanding and presents an incomplete picture of SCRes. Therefore, we conducted a systematic literature review (SLR) to advance SCRes knowledge through the theoretical lens of grand theory (GT). A total of 102 SCRes relevant, high-quality journal papers published between 2004 and 2023 were selected to synthesize existing knowledge and identify future research directions. Our study makes several novel contributions to existing SCRes knowledge. First, we believe that SCRes is determined by interactions between micro-level individuals, meso-level organizations, and macro-level environments. Thus, this study differs from existing SCRes studies by understanding it from the individual, organizational, and supply chain perspectives. Second, from the macro-level perspective, we conclude that SCRes is influenced by social, economic, technological, policy, and cultural environments. Third, from the micro-level perspective, employees' learning orientation, risk perceptions, self-leadership, and trust may impact on organizational resilience and SCRes. Finally, this study is one of first to apply GT to extend existing SCRes knowledge. We also suggest future research directions advancing SCRes knowledge.

Keywords: Supply chain resilience · micro-level individuals · meso-level organizations · macro-level environments · systematic literature review · grand theory

S. P. Duarte et al. (Eds.): ICDSST 2024, LNBIP 506, pp. 3–14, 2024.
https://doi.org/10.1007/978-3-031-59376-5_1

1 Introduction

Supply chain resilience (SCRes) has attracted significant scholarly and practitioner attention owing to its effective role in helping supply chains to prepare, respond, recover, and adapt to various crises, challenges, risks, and uncertainties [1]. Its development in the area of supply chain management (SCM) can be traced back to the early 2000s, when SCRes was defined as "the ability of a system to return to its original state or move to a new, more desirable state after being disturbed" [2]. However, resilience had already been well explored in other areas. For example, psychologists defined individual resilience as successfully adapting to life difficulties or mental problems, sociologists investigated resilient communities after setbacks, and material scientists explored objects' resilience to return to their original shape after being deformed [3]. Resilience, as a desirable characteristic of objects, individuals, and societies, has also been widely investigated in the area of business and management. For example, studies of SCRes have explored resilience capabilities [4], mitigation of supply chain risks by linking SCRes capabilities [5], resilience mitigation strategies [6], SCRes theory revolution [7], and SCRes performance assessment [8].

The variety of research interests contributes to the fragmented nature of SCRes, limiting understanding and hampering progress in this area. Recent literature reviews of SCRes published in reputable journals, such as [9] call for a more solid understanding of SCRes by re-examining relevant concepts, capabilities, and assessment measures to understand how SCRes can be maintained and improved over time. A bibliometric analysis of 771 SCRes papers published between 1988 and 2020 [10] reveals that five areas have received considerable scholarly attention: conceptual development and network design for SCRes, risk assessment to avoid supply chain breakdowns, measuring SCRes to enhance supply chain performance, utilizing resilience capabilities with other supply chain dimensions, and developing robustness in supply chain networks. However, few studies have considered how SCRes is built from a systems perspective. Deep knowledge of a supply chain system's ability to bounce back cannot be gained without a holistic understanding that links the elements involved in supply chains [11, 42–44].

Thus, in this study we conduct a systematic literature review (SLR) through the theoretical lens of grand theory (GT) to advance SCRes. GT is a social science approach that aims to explain social phenomenon by linking all levels of social reality. The more of reality to be examined, the more "grand" is the theory [12]. Our research question is: what forces from the micro-level of individuals, the meso-level of organizations, and the macro-level of environments can be used to determine SCRes? To answer this question, we thoroughly examined relevant high-quality journal papers published between 2004 and 2023. Our study makes several contributions to existing knowledge of SCRes. First, we contribute to understanding SCRes not only from the widely discussed organizational and supply chain perspectives, but also from the micro-level of individuals and the macro-level of environments. SCRes is the result of interactions between micro-level individuals, meso-level organizations, and macro-level environments. Second, this study summarizes research gaps and identifies potential future research directions by synthesizing 102 journal papers relevant to SCRes. Third, we contribute to GT by taking external environments, such as social, economic, cultural, technological, and policy, into consideration, whereas existing studies consider SCRes only from the individual, organizational, and supply chain perspectives.

In the remainder of this paper, in Sect. 2 we explain the theoretical foundation for this study, and in Sect. 3 we present our research methodology. In Sect. 4 we analyze the characteristics of papers and themes relevant to the research question, and discuss these further in Sect. 5. Finally, in Sect. 6 we draw some conclusions.

2 Grand Theory

GT refers to conceptual frameworks, models, and developments used to provide overall explanations of a discipline or body of knowledge. It seeks to link micro-, meso-, and macro-levels of social reality, and connects concepts and relationships to explain a large social landscape, and is thus useful for knowledge development [12]. We adopted GT in this study for two reasons. First, as highlighted by several previous literature reviews, GT has seldom been used to explore SCM issues. For example, one paper states that 12 theories are widely used to explore purchasing and supply management issues, but GT is rarely applied [13]. A similar conclusion is reached from a review of 411 papers published in six top SCM journals between 2009 and 2019 [14]. The results indicate that 15 theories are frequently used, including game theory, contingency theory, and organizational theory, and the authors suggest 30 theories (e.g., boundary-spanning theory and role theory) that might promote SCM research. However, these do not include GT. GT is widely applied to investigate societal and nursing issues and used to describe the true state of affairs in all settings. For example, [45] has applied GT to explore international relations and foreign policy. Second, existing studies of SCRes are fragmented and specialist in nature, lacking a broad vision of how SCRes is formulated and influenced by the elements involved. Thus, in this study, we conduct an SLR to understand how SCRes is determined by linking micro-level individuals, meso-level organizations, and macro-level environments.

3 Systematic Literature Review Methodology

An SLR was selected as the methodology for this study for several reasons. First, this novel research aims to examine forces from the micro-level of individuals, the meso-level of organizations, and the macro-level of environments that might be used to determine SCRes. An SLR is suited to overcoming the fragmented nature of SCRes by exhaustively searching for relevant journal papers in a systematic and transparent way [5]. Second, SLR are widely used to explore SCRes issues by synthesizing previous knowledge, strengthening the knowledge foundation, and identifying valuable potential research directions [8–10]. Their wide application provided us with confidence that we could use this effective tool to answer our research question. Third, the steps involved in conducting an SLR are scientific, replicable, and systematic, thereby helping to reduce bias and generating high-quality results [15]. The SLR implemented in this study includes three steps: (1) formulation of research questions; (2) identification, selection, and evaluation of studies; and (3) analysis and synthesis of the results.

3.1 Formulation of Research Questions

SCRes is widely discussed, and various definitions have been suggested. For example, it has been defined as "the ability of a system to return to its original state, within an acceptable period of time, after being disturbed" [16]. One study, based on a review of 91 SCRes papers defines SCRes in terms of complex adaptive systems theory as "the adaptive capacity of a supply chain to prepare for and/or respond to disruptions, to make a timely and cost-effective recovery, and therefore progress to a post-disruption state of operations – ideally, a better state than prior to the disruption" [17]. Our initial impression was that all scholars consider SCRes as a systems phenomenon. To confirm this, we checked several literature review papers on SCRes [8–10] and discussed the issue with two professors in operations management. The discussion corroborated that a deep knowledge of SCRes might be obtained by re-understanding it from a systems perspective. Supply chains are complex systems involving individuals and organizations, both of which are influenced by external environments. Based on this, we formulated our research question to consider interactions: what forces from the micro-level of individuals, the meso-level of organizations, and the macro-level of environments can be used to determine SCRes?

3.2 Identification, Selection, and Evaluation of Studies

To gain insights into SCRes, we selected four databases - Web of Science, Science Direct, Business Source Complete, and Emerald Insight to search for relevant, high-quality journal papers because of their wide coverage of business and management journals and frequent use by scholars to conduct SCM literature reviews. We selected a publication timespan of 2004 to 2023 because SCRes began to attract research attention following the publication of an influential study entitled "Building the Resilient Supply Chain" in *The International Journal of Logistics Management* in 2004 [2]. Consistent with previous reviews of SCRes [5, 8–10], 11 keywords were combined and searched for in titles, keywords, and abstracts: ("resilience" OR "resiliency" OR "resilient" OR "robustness" OR "mitigation") AND ("supply chain" OR "supply chains" OR "supply chain management" OR "operations management" OR "supply network" OR "supply"). The initial search produced 3,032 journal papers in English from the four selected databases. We then applied criteria to reduce the number of papers for further analysis. First, as we conducted this review mainly from a business and management perspective, we limited the search categories to management, operations research, management science, and business. This left 1,430 papers. Second, we required the selected papers to have been published in high-quality journals, as defined by the Chartered Association of Business Schools (CABS) in 2021. Therefore, only papers published in journals rated 3, 4, or 4* by CABS 2021 were included for further analysis resulting in 722 papers published in 33 journals, including *Journal of Operations Management, Journal of Supply Chain Management, Production and Operations Management,* and *Journal of Business Logistics*). Finally, we recruited three PhD students with interests in SCRes to check each paper's title, abstract, introduction, and conclusion, and remove papers irrelevant to SCRes, including purely mathematical modelling papers, and supply chain risk assessment papers. This resulted in 102 papers for further analysis.

3.3 Analysis and Synthesis of Results

Thematic analysis was employed to generate SCRes themes. This method was selected because it is useful for summarizing the key features of a large dataset, is a highly flexible and transparent process, and generates unanticipated insights [18]. The three PhD students were asked to code each paper using NVivo 13, and identify and categorize themes. We then synthesized the results and identified potential future research directions.

4 Literature Analysis

This section examines how SCRes can be determined by synthesizing existing studies and categorizing themes into the micro-level of individuals, the meso-level of organizations, and the macro-level of environments based on grand theory. We then present our theoretical framework, which open avenues for future research.

4.1 SCRes Forces Relevant to the Meso-Level of Organizations

First, we discuss capabilities that might be used to build SCRes from the meso-level of organizations because this topic is already well-developed. Prior to this, it is necessary to explore organizational resilience, which has laid the foundation for SCRes. Numerous understandings of organizational resilience are suggested. For example, one paper proposes that organizations may implement different strategies to achieve organizational resilience [19], such as, training and simulation in the preparedness phase, effective communications across supply chain stakeholders and evaluation of supply chain disruption outreach in the response phase, and maintaining employee support, continuity risk and resilience management, and reviewing the resilience strategies adopted in the recovery phase. By adopting these organizational strategies, resilience capabilities such as vertical and horizontal collaboration, supply chain re-engineering, agility, risk awareness, and knowledge management, can be achieved across the supply chain. Another paper highlights that organizational resilience depends on several critical aspects, including materials and networking, learning and culture, investment finance and cash flow, leadership, and strategic and operational flexibility [20]. In a literature review that systematically summarizes organizational resilience, it is argued that resilient behaviour, resilience resources, and resilience capabilities enable organizations to respond to disruptions [21]. As a result of learning and adapting from past disruptions, and renewing their existing resource and capability configurations, organizations can continue to strengthen their resilience.

Amongst diverse scholarly understandings of SCRes, several principles are widely viewed as building SCRes, including supply chain re-engineering, supply chain collaboration, agility, and a supply chain risk management (SCRM) culture. Within these, various capabilities are identified such as flexibility, redundancy, trust, information sharing, visibility, velocity, leadership, and innovation [20]. For example, horizontal collaboration amongst producers and vertical collaboration between processors and retailers may mitigate supply, demand, process, and control risks [22]. Several useful resilience strategies can be used at the supply chain level, including multiple suppliers, collaboration with supply chain partners, supply chain mapping, backup transportation, and flexible network design [23]. One paper presents a new understanding of how to strengthen SCRes, based on a case study of JD.com [24]. The results indicate that support provided by digital platforms, coordinating with suppliers, promoting projects to reduce unhealthy inventories, redistributing logistics networks, modifying processes for last-mile delivery, and taking social responsibility have been essential in helping supply chains to recover from the COVID-19 pandemic. A study involving semi-structured interviews in multiple industries concludes that Industry 4.0 technologies strengthen SCRes and leverage competitive advantage for supply chains [25].

Amongst several SCRes research streams, the first is Industry 4.0 technology-enabled SCRes. Keywords relevant to this stream include digital technologies, Industry 4.0 and specific relevant technologies (e.g., big data analytics, blockchain, and artificial intelligence), and technological capabilities. For example, the internet of things is said to be an effective tool for managing supply chain risks because it contributes to process transparency and management [26]. The second stream is mitigation of supply chain risks by employing SCRes capabilities. Relevant keywords include antecedents, capabilities, collaboration, robustness, innovativeness, culture, trust, visibility, and agility. The third stream links SCRes with other terms, including sustainability, Industry 5.0, and disruptions such as COVID-19. The fourth relates to discussion of the conceptual development of and pathways to SCRes [27, 28]. The fifth examines supply chain risk assessment to provide foundations for building SCRes, and the sixth evaluates SCRes capabilities, factors, or enablers for effective allocation of resources.

4.2 Impact of SCRes Forces from the Macro-Level Environments

At the meso-level of organizations, various SCRes themes have been investigated. However, very few studies have explored SCRes from the perspective of the external environment, as highlighted by a recent review of the literature on organizational resilience and SCRes [9]. From a review of 399 papers and book chapters published between 1977 and 2014, it is concluded that few insights have been gained into how to build SCRes beyond the organizational level of analysis. Therefore, more studies of industrial, policy, and societal factors that might promote SCRes are required. According to two studies, SCRes is a systems phenomenon, and should thus be understood from a systems perspective by linking individuals, organizations, and supply chains [37, 38]. However, these papers neglect to address understanding of SCRes from the external environment perspective, for instance as a socio-ecological system. Nevertheless, several studies consider environmental factors that may influence SCRes. For example, the result of an exploration of the role of a country's cultural value orientation on SCRes building in the context of COVID-19 indicate that a hierarchical cultural value orientation contributes to building resilience in supply chains, whereas an egalitarianism cultural value orientation contributes to organizational resilience building [1]. In the belief that external environments may help to achieve SCRes, one study assesses the impact of social capital on SCRes using data collected from 265 Turkish firm [29]. The results indicate that social capital has a positive effect on SCRes, mediated by absorptive capacity and marketing-SCM alignment. Another study indicates that environmental taxes may have positive effects on green technology adoption, and that the latter may foster SCRes [30]. In dynamic environments with unavoidable disruptions, establishing a resilient supply chain depends on both internal and external resilience [31]. Internal resilience refers to organizational resilience, whereas external resilience refers to the resilience of supply chain stakeholders and society. Based on data from 185 Chinese manufacturers, one study finds that SCRes may be positively impacted by the joint effects of social control and green supply chain management practices [32]. Finally, it is suggested that normative pressures stemming from professional and industry associations may force organizations to adopt big data analytics [33], and the latter has positive effects in establishing resilient supply chains [34].

4.3 Impact of SCRes Forces from the Micro-Level of Individuals

SCRes from the micro-level perspective of individuals has received little scholarly attention. Organizations and supply chains exhibit resilience because individuals are able to implement various resilience strategies. For example, knowledge management practices and a risk management culture may be critical for building SCRes [35]. Thus, regular meetings with supply chain stakeholders to acquire knowledge, special training programs to enable employees to analyze and understand newly acquired knowledge, and consistently applying new knowledge to solve operational problems are essential. It is suggested that a multilevel understanding of SCRes should be developed, including individual-, organizational-, and supply chain-levels [36]. At the individual level, individuals' learning orientation, employees' trusting disposition, and self-leadership may affect organizational resilience and SCRes. Individuals' perceptions of risk should also be taken into consideration when seeking to understand SCRes from an individual perspective [37].

4.4 A Theoretical Model of SCRes Ecosystem

Based on our review of relevant SCRes papers, we build a theoretical framework to understand SCRes from a systems perspective by linking the micro-level of individuals, the meso-level of organizations, and the macro-level of environments (see Fig. 1). At the macro-level, we believe that external environments, such as social, economic, policy, technological, and cultural environments, may influence individuals' behaviour, and thus impact on organizational resilience and SCRes building. For example, France's egalitarianism and intellectual autonomy cultural value orientation may make individuals more willing to collaborate with others and interested in joining voluntary groups, with positive effects for supply chain knowledge mobilization [4]. Organizations' and supply chains' adoption of Industry 4.0 technologies maybe driven by policy [39]. At the meso-level, organizations exhibit resilience in adopting different strategies in response to changes in the external environments. When organizations begin to share information, knowledge, and finance and collaborate with other organizations, the whole supply chain may develop resilience capabilities in the face of disruptions. Both organizations and supply chains become resilient as a result of employees' actions within each organization. Thus, at the micro-level, employees are affected by the external environment and organizational strategies. Employees who show willingness to share knowledge, build trusting relationships with others, and establish self-leadership and accurate risk perceptions, will contribute to organizational resilience and SCRes establishment.

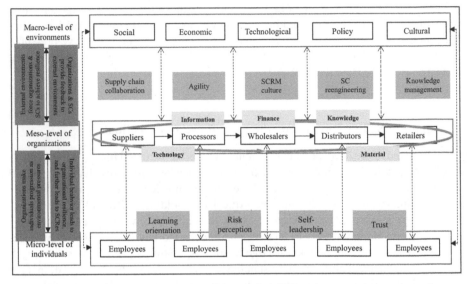

Fig. 1. A theoretical framework for understanding SCRes from a systems perspective

5   Discussion

In this study, we adopt GT to re-understand SCRes by linking the micro-level of individuals, the meso-level of organizations, and the macro-level of environments. We thus make several theoretical contributions. First, previous studies explore SCRes mainly from a meso-level perspective to identify various SCRes principles, capabilities, and capability factors that can be applied at the organizational level, such as adoption of Industry 4.0 technologies, a SCRM culture, information sharing across organizations, and redundancy [1, 5, 20]. A few studies [36, 38] call for more research to understand SCRes at individual, organizational, and supply chain levels, but neglect to appreciate that SCRes can also be influenced by the external environment. In our study, we consider that organizational and supply chain levels can be incorporated into a grand organizational level because supply chains consist of networks of relevant organizations with close connections. Thus, our study complements existing SCRes research by understanding SCRes from the environmental as well as organizational and individual perspectives. Second, this study appears to be the first to explore SCRes using GT. Previous studies focusing on SCRes make conceptual advance by utilizing dynamic theory [27], applying information processing theory to understand the moderating effects of supply chain disruptions on performance outcomes [40], or adopting a contingent resource-based view to understand how contingencies can support or hinder organizational resilience [41]. However, GT seems to be neglected. This study takes an initial step toward applying GT and illustrates that successful SCRes relies on interactions between micro-level individuals, meso-level organizations, and macro-level environments. Third, in this study we find that the external environments, including social, economic, policy, technological, and cultural environments, and individual factors such as learning orientation, self-leadership, risk perceptions, and trust may influence the establishment of organizational resilience and SCRes.

We identify several potential directions for future SCRes research. First, this study differs from existing studies that understand SCRes from the individual, organizational, and supply chain levels. In our view, SCRes depends on interactions between micro-level individuals, meso-level organizations, and macro-level environments. However, the question of which forces originating from the micro- and macro-levels may influence SCRes building remains unsolved. For example, in this study, we conclude that social, economic, technological, policy, and cultural environments may impact on SCRes building. However, the literature does not clarify how these macro-level forces may influence individuals, and thereby foster organizational resilience and further trigger SCRes. To gain a holistic understanding of SCRes, it is necessary to link the micro, meso, and macro-levels. Thus, future studies might explore which individual- and environmental-level forces may influence organizational resilience and shape SCRes, and how they do so. Second, existing studies devote attention to developing SCRes from the organizational perspective, but offer little insight into interactions between organizational resilience and SCRes. For example, how does an organization trigger SCRes after it has built its own resilience? What practices should organizations adopt to trigger resilience at the supply chain level? Further empirical research is required on the mechanisms between organizational resilience and SCRes. Third, employees are critical for organizational resilience development. However, less understood is what practices employees should adopt to achieve resilience at the organizational and then the supply chain level. Empirical studies are needed to understand the relationship between individual practices, organizational resilience strategies, and SCRes capabilities.

6 Conclusion

In this study, we systematically selected 102 high-quality journal papers from four different databases to re-analyze and deepen understanding of SCRes. Through the theoretical lens of GT, this study contributes to understanding SCRes by linking micro-level individuals, meso-level organizations, and macro-level environments, rather than focusing simply on individuals, organizations, and supply chains.

Although we adopted a rigorous research methodology, this study has several limitations that might be tackled in future research. First, we only considered high-quality journal papers published in CABS 2021 rated 3, 4, and 4* journals. Therefore, important SCRes studies published as conference proceedings or book chapters may have been overlooked. To tackle this issue, future studies might include relevant conference papers and books to generate a more comprehensive understanding of SCRes. Second, we considered journal papers from four databases and believed to cover the widest range of business and management publications worldwide, but important publications not included in these databases may have been omitted. Thus, future studies might consider other databases, such as Taylor & Francis Online, IEEE Xplore, and Proquest

Business Collection. Third, 11 keywords were used in this study to extract relevant journal papers. However, other keywords closely connected with SCRes were not included, such as keywords relating to the four SCRes phases of anticipation, resistance, response and recovery, and adaptation. Future studies might include more SCRes keywords in selecting publications for analysis.

Acknowledgement. The authors would like to acknowledge that the research leading to these results has received funding from the Ministry of Higher Education, Research and Innovation (MoHERI) of the Sultanate of Oman under the Block Funding Program. MoHERI Block Funding Agreement No MoHERI/BFP/RGP/EI/23/234.

References

1. Zhao, G., et al.: Agri-food supply chain resilience strategies for preparing, responding, recovering, and adapting in relation to unexpected crisis: a cross-country comparative analysis from the COVID-19 pandemic. J. Bus. Logist. **45**(1), e12361 (2024)
2. Christopher, M., Peck, H.: Building the resilient supply chain. Int. J. Logist. Manag. **15**(2), 1–14 (2004)
3. Adger, W.: Social and ecological resilience: are they related? Prog. Hum. Geogr. **24**(3), 347–364 (2000)
4. Zhao, G., et al.: Modelling enablers of building agri-food supply chain resilience: Insights from a comparative analysis of Argentina and France. Prod. Plan. Control **35**(3), 283–307 (2024)
5. Zhao, G., et al.: Links between risk source identification and resilience capability building in agri-food supply chains: a comprehensive analysis. IEEE Trans. Eng. Manag. (2022). https://doi.org/10.1109/TEM.2022.3221361
6. Um, J., Han, N.: Understanding the relationships between global supply chain risk and supply chain resilience: the role of mitigation strategies. Supply Chain Manag. **26**(2), 240–255 (2021)
7. Pettit, T.J., et al.: The evolution of resilience in supply chain management: a retrospective on ensuring supply chain resilience. J. Bus. Logist. **40**(1), 56–65 (2019)
8. Han, Y., et al.: A systematic literature review of the capabilities and performance metrics of supply chain resilience. Int. J. Prod. Res. **58**(15), 4541–4566 (2020)
9. Linnenluecke, M.K.: Resilience in business and management research: a review of influential publications and a research agenda. Int. J. Manag. Rev. **19**, 4–30 (2017)
10. Shishodia, A., Sharma, R., Rajesh, R., Munim, Z.H.: Supply chain resilience: a review, conceptual framework and future research. Int. J. Logist. Manag. **34**(4), 879–908 (2023)
11. Wieland, A., Durach, C.F.: Two perspectives on supply chain resilience. J. Bus. Logist. **42**(3), 315–322 (2021)
12. Turner, J.H., Boyns, D.E.: The Return of Grand Theory. In Turner, J.H (eds.) Handbook of sociological theory. Handbooks of sociology and social research. Boston, MA: Springer (2001). https://doi.org/10.1007/0-387-36274-6_18
13. Spina, G., et al.: Assessing the use of external grand theories in purchasing and supply management research. J. Purch. Supply Manag. **22**, 18–30 (2016)
14. Gligor, D., et al.: A look into the past and future: theories within supply chain management, marketing and management. Supply Chain Manag. **24**(1), 170–186 (2019)
15. Williams, R.I., Jr.: Re-examining systematic literature review in management research: additional benefits and execution protocols. Eur. Manag. J. **39**(4), 521–533 (2021)

16. Brandon-Jones, E., et al.: A contingent resource-based perspective of supply chain resilience and robustness. J. Supply Chain Manag. **50**(3), 55–73 (2014)
17. Tukamuhabwa, B.R., et al.: Supply chain resilience: definition, review and theoretical foundations for further study. Int. J. Prod. Res. **53**(18), 5592–5623 (2015)
18. Braun, V., Clarke, V.: Using thematic analysis in psychology. Qual. Res. Psychol. **3**(2), 77–101 (2006)
19. Scholten, K., Scott, P.S., Fynes, B.: Mitigation processes – antecedents for building supply chain resilience. Supply Chain Manag. **19**(2), 211–228 (2014)
20. Kamalahmadi, M., Parast, M.M.: A review of the literature on the principles of enterprise and supply chain resilience: major findings and directions for future research. Int. J. Prod. Econ. **171**, 116–133 (2016)
21. Hillmann, J., Guenther, E.: Organizational resilience: a valuable construct for management research? Int. J. Manag. Rev. **23**, 7–44 (2021)
22. Leat, P., Revoredo-Giha, C.: Risk and resilience in agri-food supply chains: the case of the ASDA PorkLink supply chain in Scotland. Supply Chain Manag. **18**(2), 219–231 (2013)
23. Gebhardt, M., et al.: Increasing global supply chains' resilience after the COVID-19 pandemic: empirical results from a Delphi study. J. Bus. Res. **150**, 59–72 (2022)
24. Shen, Z.M., Sun, Y.: Strengthening supply chain resilience during COVID -19: a case study of JD.com. J. Oper. Manag. **69**(3), 359–383 (2023)
25. Ralston, P., Blackhurst, J.: Industry 4.0 and resilience in the supply chain: A driver of capability enhancement or capability loss? Int. J. Prod. Res., **58**(16), 5006–5019 (2020)
26. Birkel, H.S., Hartmann, E.: Internet of things – the future of managing supply chain risks. Supply Chain Manag. **25**(5), 535–548 (2020)
27. Chowdhury, M.M.H., Quaddus, M.: Supply chain resilience: conceptualization and scale development using dynamic capability theory. Int. J. Prod. Econ. **188**, 185–204 (2017)
28. Van Hoek, R.: Research opportunities for a more resilient post-COVID-19 supply chain – closing the gap between research findings and industry practice. Int. J. Oper. Prod. Manag. **40**(4), 341–355 (2020)
29. Golgeci, I., Kuivalainen, O.: Does social capital matter for supply chain resilience? The role of absorptive capacity and marketing-supply chain management alignment. Ind. Mark. Manag. **84**, 63–74 (2020)
30. Shen, B., et al.: Green technology adoption in textiles and apparel supply chains with environmental taxes. Int. J. Prod. Res. **59**(14), 4157–4174 (2021)
31. Mohammed, A., et al.: COVID-19 pandemic disruption: a matter of building companies' internal and external resilience. Int. J. Prod. Res. **61**(8), 2716–2737 (2023)
32. Zhang, M., et al.: Examining green supply chain management and financial performance: roles of social control and environmental dynamism. IEEE Trans. Eng. Manag. **66**(1), 20–34 (2019)
33. Dubey, R., et al.: Big data and predictive analytics and manufacturing performance: Integrating institutional theory, resource-based view and big data culture. Br. J. Manag. **30**, 341–361 (2019)
34. Bag, S., et al.: Roles of innovation leadership on using big data analytics to establish resilient healthcare supply chains to combat the COVID-19 pandemic: a multimethodological study. IEEE Trans. Eng. Manag. (2021). https://doi.org/10.1109/TEM.2021.3101590
35. Ali, I., et al.: Achieving resilience through knowledge management practices and risk management culture in agri-food supply chains. Supply Chain Manag. **28**(2), 284–299 (2023)
36. Adobor, H.: Supply chain resilience: a multi-level framework. Int. J. Logist. Res. **22**(6), 533–556 (2019)
37. Martin, W., et al.: The role of risk perceptions in the risk mitigation process: the case of wildfire in high risk communities. J. Environ. Manag. **91**(2), 489–498 (2009)

38. Scholten, K., et al.: Dealing with the unpredictable: supply chain resilience. Int. J. Oper. Prod. Manag. **40**(1), 1–10 (2020)
39. Reischauer, G.: Industry 4.0 as policy-driven discourse to institutionalize innovation systems in manufacturing. Technol. Forecast. Soc. **132**, 26–33 (2018)
40. Wong, C.W.Y., et al.: Supply chain and external conditions under which supply chain resilience pays: An organizational information processing theorization. Int. J. Prod. Econ. (2020). https://doi.org/10.1016/j.ijpe.2019.107610
41. Parast, M.M.: Toward a contingency perspective of organizational and supply chain resilience. Int. J. Prod. Econ. (2022). https://doi.org/10.1016/j.ijpe.2022.108667
42. Ali, I., Golgeci, I.: Where is supply chain resilience research heading? a systematic and co-occurrence analysis. Int. J. Phys. Distrib. Logist. Manag. **49**(8), 793–815 (2019)
43. Kochan, C.G., Nowicki, D.R.: Supply chain resilience: a systematic literature review and typological framework. Int. J. Phys. Distrib. Logist. Manag. **48**(8), 842–865 (2018)
44. Negri, M., et al.: Integrating sustainability and resilience in the supply chain: a systematic literature review and a research agenda. Bus. Strategy. Environ. **30**(7), 2858–2886 (2021)
45. Eriksson, J.: On the policy relevance of grand theory. Int. Stud. Perspect. **15**, 94–108 (2014)

A Tool to Support Propensity Score Weighting for Enhanced Causal Inference in Business Processes

Pavlos Delias[1]([✉]), Dimitrios Trygoniaris[2], and Nikolaos Mittas[1]

[1] Democritus University of Thrace, Kavala, Greece
pdelias@af.ihu.gr, nmittas@chem.ihu.gr
[2] Aristotle University of Thessaloniki, Thessaloniki, Greece
dtrygoni@physics.auth.gr

Abstract. Effectively evaluating the impact of process interventions on business outcomes is crucial for assessing the effectiveness and return on investment of process improvement initiatives. However, this task is challenging due to the complex interplay of factors influencing process execution and performance. This paper presents a comprehensive and versatile tool that combines propensity score weighting and event logs to enhance causal inference in business processes. Propensity score weighting balances the treatment and control groups based on their observed characteristics, mitigating bias and improving the precision of causal estimates. Event logs are the input source of process mining methods, which enable the analysis and understanding of how a process works. Our tool assists practitioners in selecting the most suitable weighting method, assessing treatment-control group balance, and evaluating covariate balance before and after adjustments. We apply the approach and tool to a synthetic dataset, demonstrating their effectiveness and illustrating key insights gleaned from the analysis. We discuss the implications and benefits of this approach for advancing causal inference in business processes, alongside limitations and potential future developments for the tool.

Keywords: Business Process Improvement · Propensity Score Weighting · Process Mining · Causal Inference

1 Introduction

In the ever-evolving landscape of business process improvement, companies strive for ongoing excellence by investing resources to enhance efficiency, deliver superior customer experiences, and streamline operations. Amid these efforts, accurately measuring the true impact of process interventions becomes imperative [6,7,18]. Modern business complexities often obscure crucial questions surrounding the success factors of these process improvement initiatives, adding complexity to decision-making [26,27].

Our research tackles this challenge by seamlessly integrating two potent methodologies: propensity score weighting and process mining. Propensity

© The Author(s), under exclusive license to Springer Nature Switzerland AG 2024
S. P. Duarte et al. (Eds.): ICDSST 2024, LNBIP 506, pp. 15–30, 2024.
https://doi.org/10.1007/978-3-031-59376-5_2

scores, predicting the probability of someone undergoing a treatment based on their characteristics, have become indispensable tools for researchers figuring out cause-and-effect relationships [12]. When coupled with weighting, they enhance precision by including a broader set of observations in the analysis and facilitating a insightful understanding of group balance [2].

The benefits of propensity score weighting are substantial. Unlike matching, which involves selecting specific data points, weighting considers and incorporates a wider range of observations, leading to more accurate estimates of how process changes affect outcomes. Additionally, it enables clear reporting of the balance between treatment and reference groups, offering researchers flexibility through various weighting methods [25]. Indeed, researchers have the flexibility to choose from different propensity score weighting methods, each leveraging unique features, diagnostic affordances, and reporting parameters [8]. At this juncture, there is a growing need for a comprehensive tool that guides practitioners in selecting the most appropriate approach for their analyses. Such a tool should also be equipped with interactive features and insightful visualizations, empowering users to diagnose discerning scenarios and validate analyses by effectively leveraging propensity score weighting.

Simultaneously, process mining promotes analyzing event data to understand how a process works. It's a vital tool for understanding the intricacies of how operations actually function [1]. Our approach combines propensity score weighting with the insights from process mining to give us a more comprehensive understanding of how interventions affect business processes.

Both propensity score weighting and process mining have their merits, but there's a missing piece - a tool that seamlessly combines them. Through this work, we present such a tool, leveraging event logs (the input source of process mining methods). This tool supports process analysts in accurately gauging the impact of process enhancements, interchangeably referred to as "interventions" or "treatments". Our goal extends beyond mere tool introduction; it's about arming organizations with a practical solution for making data-driven decisions, ultimately optimizing their processes. We offer a systematic approach that streamlines the workflow, aiding analysts in specifying the propensity score model, selecting appropriate weighting methods, and assessing balance before and after adjustments, along with covariates balance evaluations. This comprehensive approach aims to facilitate continuous improvement within organizations.

2   Background

2.1   Understanding Propensity Score Weighting

Propensity score weighting is a technique that can help reduce the bias caused by confounding variables in observational studies [8]. Observational studies are studies where the researcher does not have control over the assignment of the treatment or exposure of interest, such as in surveys, or retrospective analyses like business process' event log analysis. In such studies, there may be differences between the groups that receive the treatment or not, which can affect the outcome of interest. For example, suppose we want to estimate the impact of an automation tool on expediting handling times in a claims management system. We may find that claims processed with the tool are faster than those without. However, this difference may not be due to the tool alone, but also to other factors related to tool usage and cases' cycle times. These factors, known as confounding variables, introduce biases when comparing groups [14,15]. For instance, case complexity (simpler cases are automated while more complex are not) or employee experience could affect the outcomes, highlighting the need for methods to disentangle true treatment effects from confounding influences.

To address this problem, propensity score weighting uses the concept of propensity scores, which are the probabilities of receiving the treatment or exposure given the observed covariates (confounding variables) [24]. The idea is to create a weighted sample where the distribution of the covariates is balanced between the groups, so that the effect of the treatment or exposure can be isolated from the effect of the confounding variables [19]. There are different methods to estimate the propensity scores, such as logistic regression or machine learning methods. The choice of the method depends on the characteristics of the data and the research question [11]. One of the most common methods of propensity score weighting is inverse probability of treatment weighting (IPTW), which assigns weights to each observation based on the inverse of their propensity score. For example, if an observation has a high propensity score, it means that it is very likely to receive the treatment, and therefore it will receive a low weight. Conversely, if an observation has a low propensity score, it will receive a high weight. The rationale behind this method is to give more importance to the observations that are underrepresented in their group, and less importance to the ones that are over-represented. This way, the weighted sample will have a similar distribution of the covariates between the groups, and the effect of the treatment can be estimated by comparing the weighted outcomes.

However, IPTW has some limitations, such as the possibility of extreme weights, which can increase the variance of the estimates and make them unstable. To overcome this issue, there are other variants of propensity score weighting, such as stabilized weights, trimmed weights, or overlap weights. These variants aim to reduce the variability of the weights by introducing some modifications or restrictions to the IPTW method. In Sect. 3.4 we present the rationale of the weighting methods that the proposed tool implements.

As we can see, propensity score weighting is a complex and sophisticated technique that requires careful consideration of the data, the model, and the assumptions. There are several variants of propensity score weighting, each with its own advantages and disadvantages, and the choice of the best one depends on the context and the objective of the study [20]. Therefore, a tool that can support the workflow of propensity score weighting would be very useful and beneficial for the researchers who want to apply this technique in their observational studies. Such a tool could help them to estimate the propensity scores, choose the appropriate weighting method, assess the balance of the covariates, and evaluate the robustness of the results.

2.2   Process Mining Essentials

Process mining is a field of research that aims to discover, monitor, and improve business processes by analyzing data from event logs. An event log is a record of the activities that occur in a process, capturing information such as the start and end of a task, the performer of the task, the data associated with the task, etc. An event log provides a rich and objective source of information about the actual behavior and performance of a process, as opposed to the ideal or prescribed model of the process [1].

By applying various techniques and tools to the event log, process mining can offer valuable insights for business process improvement. For example, process mining can discover the process model that best describes the event log, and compare it with the expected or desired model. This can help to identify deviations, bottlenecks, rework, or compliance issues in the process. Process mining can also measure and visualize various aspects of the process, such as the frequency, duration, cost, or quality of the tasks, the resources, or the outcomes. This can help to optimize the efficiency, effectiveness, and sustainability of the process. In addition, process mining is capable of forecasting and suggesting the optimal actions or decisions for a process, utilizing historical or real-time data from an event log. This assists in improving the agility, adaptability, and dependability of the process.

In essence, process mining is a form of evidence-based business process management, as it relies on the empirical data from the event log to support the analysis and improvement of the process [22]. Process mining can be seen as an observational study, where the researcher does not intervene or manipulate the process, but only observes what happens in the process. This allows the researcher to capture the natural and realistic behavior of the process, and open pathways to infer the causal relationships between the variables of the process. However, process mining also faces some challenges and limitations, such as the quality and completeness of the event log, the complexity and variability of the process, the process domain understanding [31], or analyzing business processes involving multiple interacting entity types [5]. In this respect, a multidisciplinary and collaborative approach is beneficial to ensure the validity and usefulness of the findings.

2.3   Bridging the Gap: Why Integration Matters

Causal inference and business process improvement stand to gain considerable advantages through their integration. This study proposes the integration of propensity score weighting and process mining, presenting them as complementary techniques capable of enhancing causal inference in the context of business process improvement. Propensity score weighting, recognized for its efficacy in mitigating bias arising from confounding variables in observational studies, aligns seamlessly with process mining, a technique adept at unveiling, monitoring, and optimizing business processes through the analysis of event logs. By integrating these two methodologies, our aim is to harness their potential synergies.

The integration of propensity score weighting and process mining forms a powerful combination that exceeds the sum of its parts. Propensity score weighting, traditionally confined to observational studies, finds renewed relevance in the domain of business process analysis. Its capability to estimate the effects of process improvements complements process mining's proficiency in uncovering business process complexities. Illustrated through concrete examples, we demonstrate how this integration yields more robust and reliable insights compared to the use of each technique in isolation-whether analyzing event logs without a proper causal inference framework or applying causal inference without considering the process perspective.

To facilitate the integration of propensity score weighting and process mining, we propose the concept of a unified tool that supports propensity score weighting for event logs. This tool streamlines the workflow of an otherwise complex procedure since many different decisions should be made by process analysts when trying to estimate the effects of a process intervention. Aiming to be user-friendly and comprehensive, such a tool becomes an asset for researchers and practitioners seeking to navigate the intricacies of causal inference for business process improvement and for organizations to take actionable steps to optimize their business processes effectively.

3   Methodological Workflow and Tool Implementation

In this section, we present our approach for streamlining the workflow of analysts when they apply propensity score weighting to the observed logs of a process execution. We do so by weaving together the methodological workflow with the tangible manifestation of our tool. Illustrated in Fig. 1, the high-level workflow, captures the essence of our streamlined process in order to enable an unbiased treatment effect estimation.

Moving beyond theory, we provide a concrete demonstration of our approach by integrating screenshots and step-by-step processes of the tool's implementation, which is freely available as a web application at https://revacc.shinyapps. io/PSWeight/. Our decision to blend the methodological workflow with the tool in action aims to enhance clarity and applicability. This combined presentation, balancing theoretical foundations with real-world tool interfaces, serves to empower analysts with a user-friendly toolkit. By bridging the gap between abstract principles and practical application, our paper contributes not only to the theoretical discourse but also equips practitioners with a tangible asset for enhanced causal inference in business processes.

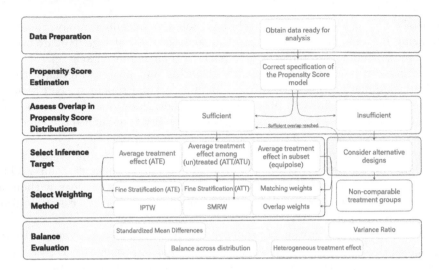

Fig. 1. The methodological workflow of propensity score weighting to enable estimating of business process intervention effects.

3.1 Data Preparation

In the initial stage of the process mining procedure, an event log $\mathcal{E}$ is utilized to document the process execution, encompassing both treated cases (those subjected to the intervention) and untreated cases (the control group). Following process mining principles, the event log typically captures activity details, timestamps, and case associations. Additionally, it may incorporate supplementary information. Leveraging the unique case identifier within the log, event data is aggregated per case identifier, resulting in a case matrix. The case matrix, denoted as $\mathbf{C}$, is structured with rows representing individual cases. Each row encompasses case-specific information, including a unique identifier, the outcome variable Y, an indication of intervention exposure A, and columns for pertinent confounding variables represented by vector $\mathbf{F}$. It is imperative to include all variables influencing the outcome to prevent model misspecification, else analysts would be left with limited recourse for correction. At the conclusion of this initial step, the matrix $\mathbf{C} = \{Y, A, \mathbf{F}\}$ is established.

To use the tool, we expect analysts to upload a case matrix $\mathbf{C}$. While offering basic functionalities, such as designating the outcome variable and indicating categorical variables (as illustrated in Fig. 3, we assume that analysts have prepared this dataset beforehand. To demonstrate the tool's functionality, we will utilize the dataset used in [6] and publicly available at [4], augmented by two randomly generated numerical variables. To facilitate comprehension, a brief overview of the example and its underlying logic from the cited work is provided herein. In particular, the causal structure of the assumed example is illustrated in Fig. 2, where it is obvious that biasing paths are open. The minimal sufficient adjustment sets for estimating the total effect of Treatment on Cycle Time should include the variables, Agent, Car Accident, Cost, New Customer, Partied Involved. To adjust for all these variables and reach a balanced distribution in both the treated as well as in the control population, we will apply propensity score weighting.

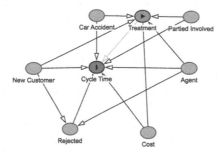

Fig. 2. The Directed Acyclic Graph reflecting the causal model of the example.

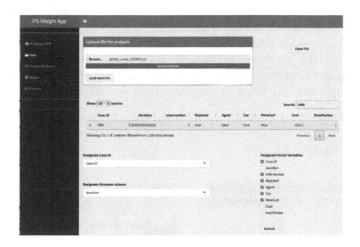

Fig. 3. Screenshot of the tool - Data Preparation Step.

3.2 Propensity Score Estimation and Assessment

Accurate propensity score estimation is pivotal in analyses utilizing this method for confounding adjustment. The tool allows three essential options to specify the propensity score model (logistic regression, generalized boosted modeling, and several machine learning techniques like k-nearest neighbors, support vector machines, regression trees) as well as it allows for custom models to be used (see Fig. 4a). Given the inherent uncertainty about the true structural relationship between treatment assignment and covariates, model misspecification is a potential concern. Various approaches, such as covariate balancing propensity scores or machine learning techniques can be explored to mitigate the risk of misspecification [10,28]. It is crucial to recognize that the impact of model misspecification may vary among different weighting approaches based on propensity scores. To address this concern, researchers can conduct a diagnostic test by assessing covariate balance between treated and reference populations before and after applying propensity score-based weights. In this step, analysts should scrutinize:

1. *Overlap*: Evaluate the extent of overlap between the treated and non-treated cases. A substantial overlap in propensity scores typically suggests a reasonable level of treatment equipoise between the two groups of cases.
2. *Positivity Violations*: Ensure that each case possesses a non-zero probability of receiving treatment. It is a fundamental assumption of propensity score analysis that the propensity score is supposed to be bounded away from zero [24].
3. *Extreme Scores*: Examine the distribution of propensity scores, considering trimming in the presence of extreme scores (close to 0 or 1). High probabilities (near 0 or 1) can lead to oversized weights, skewing the analysis by giving too much weight to cases in unusual situations who are either certain to receive the intervention or certain not to. If we exclude a substantial part of the sample by trimming regions where there's no overlap, it suggests that there isn't a sufficient overlap between the distributions. Also, cutting out observations due to non-overlapping regions can significantly change the makeup of the study group, affecting what we can infer from the results.

All these features are supported by the tool which produces visual diagnostics for both the treated and the untreated cases, via mirrored histograms, such as the one illustrated in Fig. 5a.

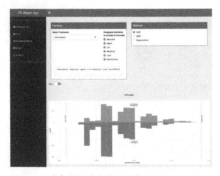
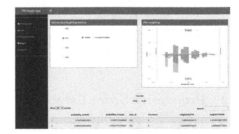

(a) Model Specification   (b) Target Estimand

Fig. 4. Screenshots of the tool, freely available at: https://revacc.shinyapps.io/PSWeight/

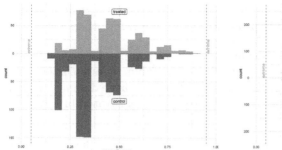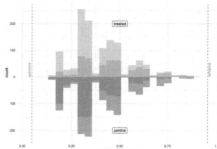

(a) Before the application of weighting.

(b) The shaded areas reflect the distribution after the weighting. Here, after IPTW considering ATE, we reach a good overlap.

Fig. 5. Mirrored histograms of the propensity score. The tool plots on the upper half the distribution of the propensity score for the treated cases and on the lower half the distribution for the untreated. The vertical dashed lines at the left and right indicate possible violations of positivity and/or extreme scores.

3.3 Select Inference Target

When estimating treatment effects, defining the appropriate estimand is crucial. The estimand represents the targeted effect within a specific population or sub-population, influencing both result interpretation and the selection of statistical methods [21].

- **Average Treatment Effect (ATE).** The ATE traditionally encompasses the entire population, treated and controlled. However, assuming all cases can transition from their current treatment to the opposite might not be scientifically sound. Careful consideration is required to ensure the chosen population aligns with the study's objectives.
- **Average Treatment Effect in the Treated (ATT).** The ATT measures treatment impact on cases mirroring those who received it in the study. It is valuable for interventions specific to certain cases characteristics or when assessing the impact of preventing harmful exposure on currently exposed cases.
- **Average Treatment Effect in the Untreated (ATU).** The ATU assesses treatment effects for a population similar to those not receiving treatment. It is valuable for deciding whether a currently unimplemented practice for some cases should persist, especially when contemplating expanding effective interventions to a group not yet receiving them.
- **Average Treatment Effect Among the Overlap Population (ATO).** The ATO assesses treatment effects in an equipoise population - where both treatments are equally implemented or there is no strong preference. Applied to cases in a state of ambiguity, the ATO is useful when intervention pro-

cedures are well understood for some cases, but uncertainty exists regarding whether treatment should be implemented or withheld for others [16].

The target population for each estimand, along with indicative research questions suitable for their application, is summarized in Table 1. As the selection of the weighting method depends on the estimand choice, we have designed a single screen for estimand and weighting method selection, as illustrated in Fig. 4b.

Table 1. Overview of estimands and the methods employed for their estimation. Adjusted from [13]

Estimand	Target population	Example research question	Weighting methods
ATE	Full sample	Should we apply the specific intervention to every eligible case?	IPTW, Fine Stratification
ATT	Treated cases	Is it advisable to stop providing the intervention to the cases currently undergoing it?	SMRW, Fine Stratification
ATU	Untreated cases	Is it advisable to broaden the intervention to include cases that are not currently receiving it?	SMRW, Fine Stratification
ATO	Equipoise	Does the intervention have an effect for some cases?	Overlap, Matching

3.4 Select Weighting Method

Propensity score weighting is a popular tool so there exist a plethora of methods [3]. In this work we have included the most popular one, considering that not all methods are suitable for all estimands.

Inverse Probability of Treatment Weighting (IPTW) [23] aims to establish a balanced pseudo-population by equalizing the distribution of covariates across treatment groups. This is accomplished by assigning weights to each case based on the inverse of its propensity score PS ($1/PS$ for the treated group and $1/(1-PS)$ for the reference group). However, it is important to note that using directly the propensity score for weighting may lead to the occurrence of extreme weights.

Fine Stratification Weights [9] do not directly employ propensity scores for weight calculation. Instead, propensity scores are utilized to construct fine strata. These strata can be created in various ways, such as using the propensity score distribution of the entire cohort or for the smaller of the two case groups. In situations where treatment is rare, forming strata based on the propensity score distribution of treated cases ensures that all treated individuals are considered, minimizing the loss of valuable information. After stratification, weights for treated and untreated cases are calculated within each stratum containing at least one treated and one untreated case. Choosing an appropriate stratification procedure to avoid sparse strata is crucial, reducing the likelihood of extreme weights, especially in situations where treatment is uncommon and the propensity score distribution is skewed. Fine stratification is versatile and applicable to both Average Treatment Effect (ATE) and Specific Treatment Effects (ATT or ATU). In the context of ATT, weights for the treated group are fixed at 1, while control cases are re-weighted according to the number of treated cases within their stratum. This ensures that control cases contribute proportionally to the overall cases within the stratum. The same principle applies to the case of ATU.

Standardized Mortality Ratio Weighting (SMRW) assigns a weight of 1 to treated cases and weights control cases based on the odds of treatment probability ($PS/(1-PS)$). SMRW also preserves the sample size of the original data and produces appropriate estimation of the variance of the main effect, addressing the issues of underestimation and inflated sample size in IPTW [29]. This method, akin to IPTW, directly employs the propensity score for weight calculation, potentially resulting in the presence of extreme weights.

Matching weights assign values based on the ratio of the lower predicted probability to the received treatment's predicted probability [30]. This method restricts weights between 0 and 1, eliminating extreme values without truncation. In equal-sized groups with good propensity score overlap, it closely estimates the ATE for the entire population. For unevenly sized groups with good overlap, it approximates the ATT in the smaller group. However, in cases of limited propensity score overlap, it focuses on estimating treatment effects within a challenging-to-evaluate subpopulation-neither the treated cases nor the entire study population.

Overlap weights (OW), similar to matching weights, are derived from predicted probabilities of receiving the opposite treatment [17]. Emphasizing observed characteristic overlap, OW continuously down-weights units in the tails of the propensity score distribution, smoothly diminishing the influence of cases at the tails without exclusions. Notably, cases with propensity scores of 0.5 contribute the most to the effect estimate, aligning with OW's focus on the population with the most treatment equipoise. This method ensures exact covariate balance without truncation, specifically focusing on estimating the Average Treatment Effect (ATE) within the overlap population, which may differ from the ATT, ATU or ATE in the entire study population.

3.5 Covariates Balance Evaluation

To ensure the validity of the causal inference and the treatment effect estimation, we need to check the balance of the covariates after applying the propensity score weighting. The balance of the covariates means that the treatment groups are similar on the observed covariates, thus eliminating the confounding bias.

We can measure the balance of the covariates using the absolute standardized difference (ASD), which is the absolute difference of the standardized means of the covariates between the treatment groups. A rule of thumb is to consider an

ASD less than 0.1 as an indication of good balance. The tool can output the ASD for each covariate in a table. However, a table may not be as intuitive and informative as a visual display. Therefore, the tool also provides three visual diagnostics to examine the balance of covariates: the *Love plot*, the *empirical cumulative distribution function* (ECDF) plot, and the *heterogeneous treatment effect* (HTE) plot (Fig. 6).

The *Love plot* shows the ASD for each covariate before and after the weighting, with different colors for each case. The plot may also show a vertical line at a specified threshold. The *Love plot* can help us to quickly identify which covariates are balanced or imbalanced, and how much the weighting improves the balance. However, the *Love plot* only shows the balance of the means of the covariates, which may not reflect the balance of the entire distributions of the covariates, especially if they are continuous.

To examine the distribution of a covariate across the treatment groups, we can use an ECDF plot. The ECDF plot shows the cumulative proportion of the covariate values grouped by the treatment groups. The ECDF plot can help us to compare the shapes and modes of the covariate distributions between the groups. If the lines of the ECDF plot are close to each other, it means that the distributions are similar. If there are gaps between the lines, it means that there are differences in the distributions that the ASD may not capture. The tool can produce the ECDF plot for each continuous covariate before and after the weighting, and show the improvement in the distributional balance. However, even if the distributions are balanced, it does not guarantee that the treatment effect is constant across the covariate space. There may be some non-linear or interaction, or other effects that the propensity score model fails to capture, leading to treatment effect heterogeneity. This means that the effect of the exposure on the outcome may vary depending on the values of the covariates.

To explore the possible treatment effect heterogeneity, the tool can create an HTE plot to see if the effect is constant across the propensity score, which is a summary of the covariate space. The HTE plot shows the outcome values grouped by the treatment. The plot also shows a regression line for each treatment group, indicating the trend of the outcome values across the propensity score values. If the lines are parallel, it means that the treatment effect is constant across the propensity score. If the lines cross (or converge or exhibit varying slopes), it means that there is treatment effect heterogeneity, and the effect may depend on the propensity score or the covariates. The tool can create the HTE plot to explore the possible treatment effect heterogeneity.

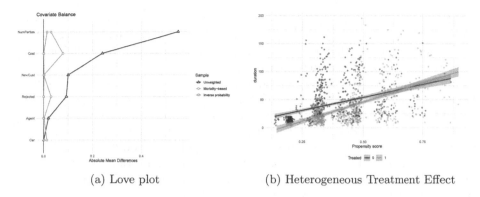

(a) Love plot   (b) Heterogeneous Treatment Effect

Fig. 6. Visual diagnostics to examine the balance of covariates

4   Conclusion

The aim of this work is to streamline the process of accurately measuring the causal impact of process interventions on business outcomes, using event logs that have recorded the process execution. This is a crucial task for organizations that want to evaluate the effectiveness of their process improvement initiatives, and to identify the best practices and strategies for achieving their goals.

The approach of integrating propensity score weighting with event logs is demonstrated by the provision of a comprehensive and flexible tool that guides practitioners in selecting the most appropriate weighting method for their analysis, assessing the balance between treatment and control groups, and evaluating the covariates balance before and after adjustments. The approach is demonstrated by applying the tool to a synthetic dataset, and showing the main findings or insights that are obtained from the analysis.

The implications and benefits of the approach for enhancing causal inference in business processes are that it enables organizations to measure the causal impact of process interventions on various business outcomes, such as customer satisfaction, revenue, costs, quality, or efficiency. It also provides analysts with a comprehensive and flexible tool that supports them in selecting the most suitable weighting method for their analysis, based on their data characteristics, causal assumptions, and inference target. The tool also assists them in assessing the balance between treatment and control groups, and in evaluating the covariates balance before and after adjustments. This can help them to ensure the validity and robustness of their causal inference, and to avoid potential biases or confounding factors that could distort their results. The approach can also help organizations to identify and address any challenges or limitations that they may face or encounter while implementing or applying the tool, such as data quality, model misspecification, or treatment effect heterogeneity.

However, two notable limitations currently characterize the tool. Firstly, its features and logic are constructed around the binary treatment assumption (there are cases that received the single version of the intervention, and cases that did not), neglecting other treatment types (e.g., multi-category treatments, continuous treatments) or input data variations (e.g., clustered data). While there are features that could potentially work with multi-category or continuous treatments, extensive testing for such scenarios remains an avenue for future exploration. Moreover, the current tool's functionality extends only up to achieving balance in the two pseudo-sub-populations, omitting the task of actually estimating treatment effects. To address this limitation, we envision an integrated decision support tool that not only facilitates the follow-up of propensity score weighting with treatment effect estimation but also allows for testing alternative approaches (e.g., matching, doubly robust methods) and comparing effect estimations. This expansion will enhance the tool's scope and provide analysts with a more comprehensive suite for robust causal inference in the field of business processes.

References

1. van der Aalst, W.: Process Mining. Springer, Berlin Heidelberg, Berlin, Heidelberg (2016). https://doi.org/10.1007/978-3-662-49851-4
2. Austin, P.C.: An introduction to propensity score methods for reducing the effects of confounding in observational studies. Multivar. Behav. Res. **46**(3), 399–424 (2011)
3. Cannas, M., Arpino, B.: A comparison of machine learning algorithms and covariate balance measures for propensity score matching and weighting. Biom. J. **61**(4), 1049–1072 (2019)
4. Delias, P.: Simulation data for Doubly Robust Estimation of Business Process Intervention (2023). https://doi.org/10.5281/ZENODO.7971636
5. Delias, P., Grigori, D.: Formulating the potentials of clustering of event data over multiple entities for decision support: a network embeddings approach. J. Decision Syst. 1–23 (2023)
6. Delias, P., Mittas, N., Florou, G.: A doubly robust approach for impact evaluation of interventions for business process improvement based on event logs. Decision Analytics J. **8**, 100291 (2023)
7. Delias, P., Nguyen, G.T.: Prototyping a business process improvement plan an evidence-based approach. Inform. Syst. **101**, 101812 (2021)
8. Desai, R.J., Franklin, J.M.: Alternative approaches for confounding adjustment in observational studies using weighting based on the propensity score: a primer for practitioners. BMJ l5657 (2019)
9. Desai, R.J., Rothman, K.J., Bateman, B.T., Hernandez-Diaz, S., Huybrechts, K.F.: A propensity-score-based fine stratification approach for confounding adjustment when exposure is infrequent. Epidemiology **28**(2), 249–257 (2017)

10. Ferri-García, R., Rueda, M.D.M.: Propensity score adjustment using machine learning classification algorithms to control selection bias in online surveys. PLoS ONE **15**(4), e0231500 (2020)
11. Fuentes, A., Lüdtke, O., Robitzsch, A.: Causal inference with multilevel data: a comparison of different propensity score weighting approaches. Multivar. Behav. Res. **57**(6), 916–939 (2022)
12. Govindarajulu, U.: Commentary on Rubin and Rosenbaum Seminal 1983 paper on propensity scores: from then to now. Observat. Stud. **9**(1), 19–22 (2023)
13. Greifer, N., Stuart, E.A.: Choosing the Causal Estimand for Propensity Score Analysis of Observational Studies (2021). publisher: arXiv Version Number: 2
14. Grimes, D.A., Schulz, K.F.: Bias and causal associations in observational research. Lancet **359**(9302), 248–252 (2002)
15. Johnson, S.R., Tomlinson, G.A., Hawker, G.A., Granton, J.T., Feldman, B.M.: Propensity score methods for bias reduction in observational studies of treatment effect. Rheumatic Disease Clin. North America **44**(2), 203–213 (2018)
16. Li, F., Morgan, K.L., Zaslavsky, A.M.: Balancing covariates via propensity score weighting. J. Am. Stat. Assoc. **113**(521), 390–400 (2018)
17. Li, F., Thomas, L.E.: Addressing extreme propensity scores via the overlap weights. Am. J. Epidemiol. (2018)
18. Lok, P., Hung, R.Y., Walsh, P., Wang, P., Crawford, J.: An integrative framework for measuring the extent to which organizational variables influence the success of process improvement programmes. J. Manage. Stud. **42**(7), 1357–1381 (2005)
19. Lunceford, J.K., Davidian, M.: Stratification and weighting via the propensity score in estimation of causal treatment effects: a comparative study. Stat. Med. **23**(19), 2937–2960 (2004)
20. Markoulidakis, A., et al.: A tutorial comparing different covariate balancing methods with an application evaluating the causal effects of substance use treatment programs for adolescents. Health Serv. Outcomes Res. Method. **23**(2), 115–148 (2023)
21. Pirracchio, R., Carone, M., Rigon, M.R., Caruana, E., Mebazaa, A., Chevret, S.: Propensity score estimators for the average treatment effect and the average treatment effect on the treated may yield very different estimates. Stat. Methods Med. Res. **25**(5), 1938–1954 (2016)
22. Reinkemeyer, L. (ed.): Process Mining in Action: Principles. Use Cases and Outlook. Springer International Publishing, Cham (2020). https://doi.org/10.1007/978-3-030-40172-6
23. Robins, J.: A new approach to causal inference in mortality studies with a sustained exposure period-application to control of the healthy worker survivor effect. Math. Model. **7**(9–12), 1393–1512 (1986)
24. Rosenbaum, P.R., Rubin, D.B.: The central role of the propensity score in observational studies for causal effects. Biometrika **70**(1), 41–55 (1983)
25. Stürmer, T., et al.: Propensity score weighting and trimming strategies for reducing variance and bias of treatment effect estimates: a simulation study. Am. J. Epidemiol. **190**(8), 1659–1670 (2021)
26. Syed Ibrahim, M., Hanif, A., Jamal, F.Q., Ahsan, A.: Towards successful business process improvement - an extension of change acceleration process model. PLoS ONE **14**(11), e0225669 (2019)
27. Trkman, P.: The critical success factors of business process management. Int. J. Inf. Manage. **30**(2), 125–134 (2010)
28. Webster-Clark, M., et al.: Using propensity scores to estimate effects of treatment initiation decisions: State of the science. Stat. Med. **40**(7), 1718–1735 (2021)

29. Xu, S., Ross, C., Raebel, M.A., Shetterly, S., Blanchette, C., Smith, D.: Use of stabilized inverse propensity scores as weights to directly estimate relative risk and its confidence intervals. Value Health **13**(2), 273–277 (2010)
30. Yoshida, K., et al.: Matching weights to simultaneously compare three treatment groups: comparison to three-way matching. Epidemiology **28**(3), 387–395 (2017)
31. Zimmermann, L., Zerbato, F., Weber, B.: Process mining challenges perceived by analysts: an interview study. In: Augusto, A., Gill, A., Bork, D., Nurcan, S., Reinhartz-Berger, I., Schmidt, R. (eds.) Enterprise, Business-Process and Information Systems Modeling, vol. 450, pp. 3–17. Springer International Publishing, Cham (2022). https://doi.org/10.1007/978-3-031-07475-2_1

MCDA Calculator: A Streamlined Decision Support System for Multi-criteria Decision Analysis

He Huang$^{(\boxtimes)}$ⓘ and Peter Burgherrⓘ

Laboratory for Energy Systems Analysis, Paul Scherrer Institute, Forschungsstrasse 111, 5232 Villigen, PSI, Switzerland
{he.huang,peter.burgherr}@psi.ch

Abstract. The multi-criteria decision analysis (MCDA) landscape is fraught with complexity and challenges, particularly in diverse decision-making environments. Practitioners often face the challenging tasks of selecting appropriate MCDA methodologies, navigating complicated computational processes, and effectively synthesizing inputs from a variety of stakeholders. The existing landscape of MCDA tools, which are typically limited to specific methodologies, exacerbates these challenges, often resulting in fragmented workflows and steep learning curves. To overcome these hurdles, the MCDA Calculator (https://mcda-calculator. psi.ch) emerges as a novel decision support system (DSS), providing a unified and streamlined platform tailored to increase the efficiency and effectiveness of computational process for experienced practitioners in applying MCDA. The MCDA Calculator features a streamlined computational workflow that blends different MCDA methodologies into a cohesive unit. This approach ensures a consistent and intuitive user experience, effectively eliminating the need for complex, time-consuming configurations. The tool's design philosophy focuses on simplifying the MCDA calculation process. In this paper, we introduce our DSS and detail the workflow of the developed web-based tool. To illustrate the practical benefits and real-world applicability of the MCDA Calculator, the paper presents a numerical example which illustrates the tool's ability to streamline calculation processes, and produce insightful, actionable results.

Keywords: Multi-criteria decision analysis · Decision support system · Software development

1 Introduction

In the field of decision making, Multi-Criteria Decision Analysis (MCDA) methods have proliferated over several decades, forming a large and diverse "family" [15]. Each member of this family has distinct characteristics that make them applicable in different contexts. The diversity of MCDA methods provides practitioners with structured and context-specific approaches to evaluate complex decision problems. Additionally, the application of these methods in

S. P. Duarte et al. (Eds.): ICDSST 2024, LNBIP 506, pp. 31–45, 2024.
https://doi.org/10.1007/978-3-031-59376-5_3

real-world scenarios necessitates an intuitive and user-friendly interaction with the data, ideally through a Decision Support System (DSS). To address this, user interface(UI)-based software solutions have been developed that streamline the decision-making process [18]. Specialized software such as PriEsT for the Analytical Hierarchy Process (AHP) [26], Visual-PROMETHEE for the PROMETHEE method [21], and ValueDecisions for the Multi-Attribute Value Theory (MAVT) [16] have been developed, each tailored to the computational nuances of different MCDA methods. Some other software solutions are developed to guide and incorporate the input of multiple decision makers (DMs), experts, and stakeholders into the decision process. This requires an instructive framework that facilitates group decision-making and provides a comprehensive view of the collective results. Software solutions such as SOCRATES for the Social Multi-Criteria Evaluation (SMCE) framework [23] and MAMCA software [17] have been developed to focus on stakeholder interaction.

Despite advances in software tools designed to facilitate the application of MCDA methods, several gaps remain, particularly in their practical utility for practitioners. While most existing software provides detailed, instructive procedures to assist practitioners unfamiliar with these methods, these guidelines can be redundant and time-consuming for those already experienced in the field. The step-by-step instructions, while beneficial for beginners, can hinder the efficiency of experienced practitioners, causing unnecessary delays in their workflow. Another challenge is the need for versatility in applying different MCDA methods to different cases. Current software solutions are often dedicated to specific MCDA methodologies, forcing practitioners to switch between software platforms. This not only disrupts the continuity of their work, but also introduces additional learning curves as each software comes with its own unique interface and operating mechanics. This fragmentation of available tools can hinder the seamless integration of different MCDA approaches into a single, streamlined process. Although tools such as Diviz offer comprehensive solutions for the different MCDA methods, their effective utilization often necessitates a solid foundation in programming or an in-depth understanding of block building methodologies [4]. These prerequisites can create barriers for practitioners who may not possess such technical expertise, limiting the accessibility and wider adoption of these otherwise powerful MCDA tools.

To fill this gap, there is a need for a comprehensive tool that integrates different MCDA methodologies while providing intuitive and straightforward usability. Such a tool should minimize trivial settings and configurations, allowing practitioners, especially MCDA experts, to focus more on analysis and less on navigating the software. It should provide a platform where multiple MCDA methodologies can be seamlessly accessed and applied, with an easy-to-use interface that appeals to both novice and experienced practitioners. This consolidation of functionality would not only increase the efficiency of MCDA application, but also enrich the decision-making process, allowing for a more holistic and flexible approach to problem-solving in different contexts.

In this paper, our objective is to improve the methodological framework for MCDA computations, focusing specifically on integration within a visualized system. We present our newly developed DSS, the MCDA Calculator web tool, which is specifically designed to encapsulate different MCDA methods and seamlessly derive computations from them. We propose a streamlined computational structure for MCDA methods that allows different methods to adhere to a uniform process flow for generating results. This approach ensures that regardless of the MCDA method used, the process remains consistent and user-friendly, thereby simplifying the application of these methods and increasing the efficiency and effectiveness of the decision-making process. The paper is organized as follows: We begin with a literature review on existing MCDA methods and compare them with our software. Next, we detail the workflow and structure of the MCDA Calculator. Finally, we demonstrate the application of our tool through a numerical example, showcasing its practical utility.

2 Literature Review: Revisiting MCDA DSS from Practical Usage

In this section, much of the discourse on Multi-Criteria Decision Analysis (MCDA) revolves around its real-world application, particularly the challenges associated with its complex computational requirements. Given the intricate nature of MCDA calculations, there is an increasing reliance on computational support. For example, it can be facilitated by libraries in various programming languages. Notable examples include the Python-based libraries [7, 30] and those in R [3]. Despite their comprehensiveness, these libraries present a significant hurdle for non-technical experts due to their lack of user-friendly interfaces and interactivity, making them less practical. Therefore, software as DSS play a critical role in bridging this gap. They help practitioners construct problem structures, implement MCDA methodologies, and visualize results in an accessible manner. Such systems offer increased convenience and flexibility in various contexts. For example, they allow practitioners to easily modify data and MCDA parameters or present results in stakeholder meetings and workshops. However, these DSSs are not without limitations. Each system has different features tailored to specific contexts. Some specialize in particular MCDA methods, while others emphasize interaction with practitioners, focus on post-hoc analysis, or are good at facilitating group decision making.

The variety of software underscores the importance of a comprehensive review to compare features and identify potential gaps. Such an analysis is critical to understanding their suitability in different decision-making scenarios. For this review, our attention is focused on MCDA DSSs with UI that have been developed within the last decade and remain accessible and operational today[1]. Given the large number of MCDA methods and software applications available, our focus will be on conducting a comparison of free (or partially free) MCDA tools for scoring and ranking. This comparative study aims to map the landscape of

---

[1] Test environment specifications: Operating System is Windows 10 and the processor is an Intel® Core™ i7-12800H.

available DSSs in MCDA, provide insights into their strengths and limitations, and identify areas where new developments could be most beneficial. Our comparative analysis focuses on the key features of different MCDA software, following the process stages proposed by Belton and Stewart [2]. These stages include problem structuring, model building, and challenging thinking. We examine and question the specific features offered by different software, focusing on how they facilitate each of these stages:

Phase 1: Problem structuring. The problem structuring phase is characterized by divergent thinking, where the focus is on mapping goals, values, and constraints while acknowledging the uncertainties and influences of external environmental factors. It is a stage where the range of stakeholders is brainstormed, along with the identification of primary alternatives and the establishment of appropriate criteria. The key features we examine are:

- $Q_{1,1}$: Does the DSS provide a heuristic approach to enable effective brainstorming for problem structuring?
- $Q_{1,2}$: Is the DSS designed to incorporate inputs from multiple actors, including stakeholders, decision-makers, or experts?

Phase 2: Model building. The model building phase marks a transition to a focused, convergent approach that synthesizes the rich insights from the problem structuring phase into defined, actionable elements of the decision process. This phase focuses on detailing alternatives, establishing criteria, and capturing associated values, preferences, and performance. We evaluate the following key features of the DSS:

- $Q_{2,1}$: Does the DSS provide a method for importing structured data to streamline the process instead of manual information entry?
- $Q_{2,2}$: Does the DSS provide weight elicitation methods (rather than directly entering the criteria weights)?
- $Q_{2,3}$: What MCDA method(s) does the DSS offer?

Phase 3: Challenging Thinking This phase brings the model results into discussion and uses critical analysis to explore the robustness of the constructed models to different scenarios and assumptions. For example, sensitivity analysis can be used to understand the impact of changes in criteria weights and alternative performance, and to assess the stability of the decision outcome. This phase ensures the robustness and reliability of the decision process. We evaluate the following key features of the DSS:

- $Q_{3,1}$: Does the DSS offer visualization tools for results to aid in discussion and interpretation?
- $Q_{3,2}$: Is there a feature within the DSS to export the results of the MCDA for further use and analysis?
- $Q_{3,3}$: Does the DSS include a module for conducting sensitivity analysis to assess the robustness of the decision outcomes?

In addition, we ask some general questions about the nature of software:

– $Q_{0,1}$: Does the platform operate as a web-based tool or is it configured for desktop installation?
– $Q_{0,2}$: Is the software open source?

The detailed comparative analysis of the MCDA DSSs is presented in Table 1.

Table 1. MCDA DSS comparison

DSS	$Q_{0,1}$	$Q_{0,2}$	$Q_{1,1}$	$Q_{1,2}$
Entscheidungsnavi [24]	Web-based	✓	✓	✗
FITradeoff [14]	Web-based	✗	✗	✗
MAMCA [17]	Web-based	✗	✗	✓
MCDA Index Tool [9]	Web-based	✗	✗	✗
PriEsT [25]	Desktop-based	✓	✗	✗
SOCRATES [23]	Web-based	✗	✗	✓
ValueDecisions [16]	Web-based	✓	✗	✓
Visual PROMETHEE [21]	Desktop-based	✗	✗	✗

DSS	$Q_{2,1}$	$Q_{2,2}$	$Q_{2,3}$
Entscheidungsnavi	JSON	✓	MAUT [12]
FITradeoff	Excel	✓	FITradeoff [13]
MAMCA	Excel	✓	AHP [28], SMART [29]
MCDA Index Tool	CSV	✓	SAW [19]
PriEsT	Special format	✓	AHP [28]
SOCRATES	JSON	✗	NAIADE [22]
ValueDecisions	Excel	✗	MAVT [5]
Visual PROMETHEE	CSV, TXT	✗	PROMETHEE [6]

DSS	$Q_{3,1}$	$Q_{3,2}$	$Q_{3,3}$
Entscheidungsnavi	✓	JSON	✓
FITradeoff	✓	Excel	✓
MAMCA	✓	Excel	✓
MCDA Index Tool	✓	CSV	✓
PriEsT	✓	Special format	✓
SOCRATES	✓	JSON	✓
ValueDecisions	✓	✗	✓
Visual PROMETHEE	✓	CSV, etc.	✓

In general, there is a trend in MCDA DSSs to move from traditional desktop-based applications to web-based tools. This shift addresses the various environmental support requirements, such as specific Java libraries, that desktop applications require. Web tools offer ease of use; a simple browser is all that is needed to launch the DSS, enabling cross-platform compatibility across PCs, mobile phones and tablets. Import and export functionality is considered essential, as evidenced by its ubiquity in all DSSs surveyed. However, the preferred formats for these functions vary, with easy-to-use options such as CSV and Excel being more common, as opposed to JSON or proprietary formats that can pose usability challenges.

In addition, it is observed that each DSS tends to specialize in different MCDA methodologies, resulting in different data entry methods and value elicitation processes. This specialization highlights the need for a tailored approach to handle the nuances of different MCDA techniques. Finally, the provision of sensitivity analysis is a notable feature, whose importance is underscored by its consistent inclusion in all DSSs. The prevalence of this feature indicates its crucial role in assessing the robustness of decision outcomes. Additionally, several DSSs also integrate group decision-making, which makes collaborative decision-making possible.

Our analysis shows that modern MCDA DSSs are equipped with comprehensive functionalities that enable a complete decision process within the software. In particular, Entscheidungsnavi provides a heuristic approach to problem structuring. However, we observe that these systems often have a steep learning curve. Typically, DSSs are limited to one or two MCDA methods, a limitation resulting from the inherent diversity of MCDA methods. As a result, practitioners may have to switch between different DSS platforms to use different MCDA methods. In addition, as shown in Fig. 1, the functional design of these DSSs varies, resulting in different workflows. Some systems adopt a linear process flow that requires step-by-step input from practitioners. While systematic, this approach can be time-consuming. Others offer a comprehensive set of functions across different sections of the interface, which, while thorough, can be confusing due to its complexity.

While the current landscape of DSSs with comprehensive MCDA capabilities is impressive, it often exceeds the needs of practitioners seeking speed and flexibility. There is a notable research gap in addressing scenarios where practitioners require fast, straightforward computations using different MCDA methods across different case studies. Existing systems, with their extensive feature sets and structured workflows, are designed more for in-depth analysis, which, while thorough, can be cumbersome for practitioners who need to quickly switch between methods and case studies. This gap highlights the need for a more agile and adaptable DSS that prioritizes efficiency and ease of use without compromising the breadth of MCDA methodologies.

3   Proposal of a Streamlined MCDA DSS: MCDA Calculator

In response to the research gap we identified, we present our proposed DSS: the MCDA Calculator. The goal is to provide a systematic and streamlined framework to assist practitioners in developing computational structure and efficiently

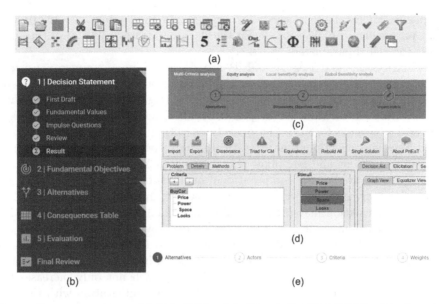

Fig. 1. Screenshots from MCDA DSSs: (a) Visual PROMETHEE; (b) Entschei-dungsnavi; (c) SOCRATES; (d) PriEsT; (e) MAMCA.

computing results using a range of MCDA methodologies according to a set of defined requirements: Through our investigation, we discovered that a certain category of MCDA methods could be effectively incorporated into a unified computational model. The defining characteristics of these MCDA methods include:

- The primary focus is on ranking problems, where the goal is to obtain a complete ordinal ranking of alternatives;
- The sets of alternatives and criteria are predetermined and fixed, ensuring a stable and consistent data structure;
- Scoring functions are applied to integrate multiple criteria, culminating in a comprehensive final ranking.

Several prominent MCDA methods, such as PROMETHEE [6], TOPSIS [1], and MAVT [5], satisfy these criteria. Thus, in our DSS, we propose a high-level computational model, denoted $\mathcal{F}$, for these MCDA methods, taking into account various parameters:

$$\mathcal{F}(\mathcal{A}, \mathcal{M}, \mathcal{P}, \mathcal{G}), \tag{1}$$

where $\mathcal{A}$ denotes the matrix of collected alternative data over different criteria. $\mathcal{M}$ is a 1-tuple that specifically indicates the chosen MCDA method. $\mathcal{P}$ is the matrix that encapsulates parameters for the criteria, such as polarity, weights of the criteria, and method-specific parameters like those used in PROMETHEE to construct preference functions. Finally, $\mathcal{G}$ symbolizes the global parameters, represented as a tuple. This can range from a 0-tuple to n-tuples, depending on the specific MCDA method used. For example, in the context of VIKOR, the global parameter v is given to define the decision strategy [20], resulting in a 1-tuple for global parameters.

To clarify, the matrices $\mathcal{A}$ and $\mathcal{P}$ are described in a manner consistent with computer science principles, accommodating a range of data types and scales, including both numeric and non-numeric (e.g., strings) elements. Their representation as matrices serves primarily to structure the data in an organized and accessible format. The operations within the computational model extend beyond conventional mathematical matrix operations to include specialized transformations and mappings relevant to each MCDA method.

The primary goal of the computational model is to provide aggregate scores for the alternatives under consideration. However, in certain MCDA methods, additional information may prove valuable. For example, in the PROMETHEE method, we encounter metrics such as negative flows, positive flows, and net flows, while TOPSIS provides distances relative to the best and worst conditions. To effectively capture and use this additional information, we propose to structure it as matrices, denoted by $\mathcal{R}$. This approach not only increases the comprehensiveness of our analysis, but also facilitates integration with the programming languages used to develop our DSS.

With the computational model in place, we now present our MCDA calculator flowchart. As shown in Fig. 2, our proposed MCDA calculator is defined by a linear workflow, but includes decision points where the practitioner must ensure that the correct data or parameters have been entered before proceeding to the next step. This ensures the accuracy and completeness of the information entered at each stage of the MCDA process.

First, practitioners import the performance data of alternatives into the data matrix $\mathcal{A}$. The DSS expects an $x \times y$ matrix, i.e., $\mathcal{A}_{x \times y}$, for a decision problem consisting of x alternatives and y criteria. If the data matrix is not properly structured, the system prompts the practitioner to adjust the data. Once the data is properly formatted, the next step is to select an appropriate MCDA method, represented by $\mathcal{M}$. After selecting the MCDA method, the practitioner must enter the necessary criteria parameters in the matrix $\mathcal{P}$ and global parameters in $\mathcal{G}$, if applicable. For an MCDA method that requires z criterion parameters, the DSS expects a $y \times z$ matrix, i.e., $\mathcal{M}_{y \times z}$. Only when all parameters are correctly filled, the system proceeds to calculate the MCDA scores by applying the model $\mathcal{F}(\mathcal{A}, \mathcal{M}, \mathcal{P}, \mathcal{G})$, and finally obtains the MCDA result matrix $\mathcal{R}$. Should practitioners or DMs find the results unsatisfactory, or if they wish to validate the performance of alternatives using different MCDA methods, they have the option to recalculate. Importantly, this can be done without re-importing all the data, streamlining the process for further analysis.

4   Development and Demonstration of the Web-Based DSS

Based on the structure outlined in the flowchart, we developed the web-based DSS, the MCDA Calculator. This application was built using Dash, a flexible and lightweight Python framework designed for building web applications [10]. The MCDA Calculator is hosted at https://mcda-calculator.psi.ch and operates as a one-page application. This design allows practitioners to experience a cohesive workflow on a single page, encompassing every step from the initial data import to the final result (see Fig. 4). Currently, the MCDA calculator includes methods like PROMETHEE, TOPSIS, VIKOR, and SMART.

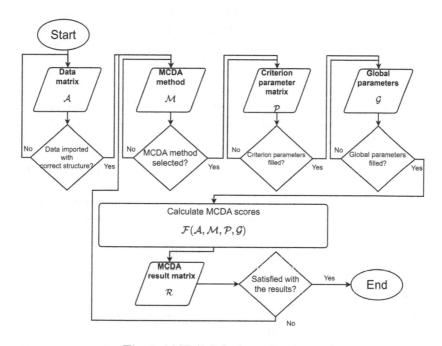

Fig. 2. MCDA Calculator flowchart

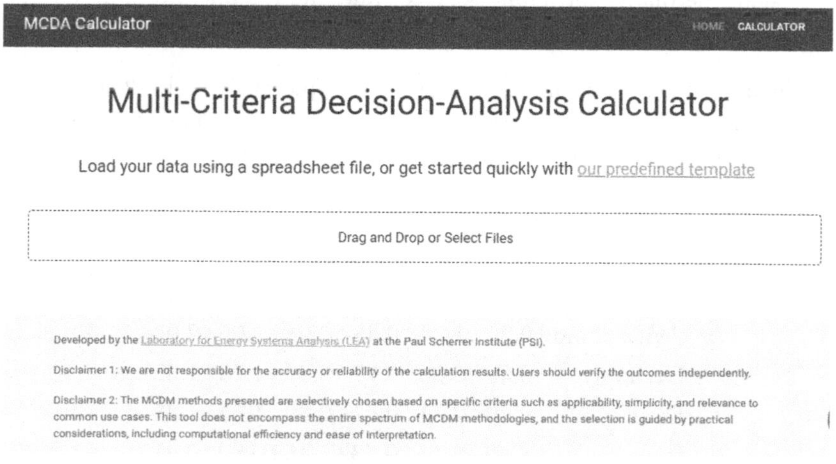

Fig. 3. Screenshot of the MCDA Calculator DSS

Given the abstract nature of the computational model, we will demonstrate the workflow of the DSS with a simplified analysis, which was originally designed as a practical exercise for master's students in energy system analysis at ETH Zurich. The case is adapted from a published work of Siskos and Burgherr [27], which analyzes the resilience of European countries' electricity supply systems. It aims to deepen the understanding of how complex and multidimensional concepts like energy system resilience can be assessed using a MCDA methodology. The exercise focuses on the evaluation of three major resilience dimensions: Resist, Restabilise, and Recover. As a simplified case study, the task involves evaluating and ranking Switzerland and its neighboring European countries based on their performance across 6 criteria (indicators) that influence their electricity supply resilience. The criteria are:

1. c_1 System Average Interruption Duration Index - SAIDI (Resist dimension): The SAIDI is a measure of the total duration of electricity supply interruptions per customer per year.
2. c_2 Political stability and absence of violence/terrorism (Resist dimension): A composite indicator that measures to what extent the political system is stable and not hindered by acts of violence and terrorism.
3. c_3 Electricity mix diversity (Restabilise dimension): This criterion measures the diversification of the electricity mix of each country, to different electricity generation technologies.
4. c_4 Electricity import dependence (Restabilise dimension): This criterion defines the ratio between electricity consumption and production in each European country.
5. c_5 Annual GDP growth (Recover dimension): A country exhibiting an expansion to its Gross Domestic Product (GDP) is expected to foster long-term investments and economic growth.
6. c_6 Government effectiveness (Recover dimension): Government effectiveness represents the quality of public services and the readiness of policy formulation and implementation.

The collected data for the alternative are depicted in Table 2. It should be noted that the majority of the indicators presented are composite indices. Consequently, specific units are not assigned to these indicators in the table.

Table 2. Data for evaluation

	c_1	c_2	c_3	c_4	c_5	c_6
Switzerland	0.20	1.34	0.43	0.98	2.05	2.04
Germany	0.30	0.60	0.77	0.92	1.93	1.62
France	0.40	0.11	0.47	0.89	1.52	1.48
Italy	1.30	0.31	0.73	1.15	0.90	0.41
Austria	0.60	0.92	0.56	1.14	1.89	1.45

To compute the resilience scores of different countries (alternatives) based on specific criteria, we will use two intuitive MCDA methods available in our DSS and demonstrate their efficient workflow. For this demonstration, we have selected methods from the Simple Multi-Attribute Rating Technique (SMART) family and the Technique for Order of Preference by Similarity to Ideal Solution (TOPSIS). Readers interested in a comprehensive explanation of these methods can refer to the existing literature [1, 11].

The first step within the DSS is to upload the data matrix $\mathcal{A}$ as described in Table 2. Practitioners have the convenience of importing data via a spreadsheet compatible with Excel or CSV formats. After importing the data, a method selection prompt appears, allowing the practitioner to select an MCDA method. When SMART is selected, the system dynamically generates parameter tables tailored for user-friendly input, allowing practitioners to populate the parameter matrix $\mathcal{P}$. For each criterion, practitioners must specify the corresponding polarity, minimum plausible parameter q_{min}, maximum plausible parameter q_{max}, and weight, as described in Table 3. As there is no global parameter in SMART, after completing this step, the DSS automatically skips this step, and practitioners can proceed to calculate the results by clicking the "Calculate the Result" button. When practitioners choose the TOPSIS method, the required parameters for $\mathcal{P}$ include the polarities of the criteria and their corresponding weights (see Table 3). There is no need for practitioners to start from scratch; they can seamlessly transition to calculating the TOPSIS results after calculating the SMART results, ensuring a smooth and efficient analysis process.

Table 3. Criterion parameters in SMART and TOPSIS method

		SMART parameters			TOPSIS parameters	
Criterion	Polarity	q_{min}	q_{max}	Weight	Polarity	Weight
c_1	Negative	0,2	1,3	0,08	Negative	0,08
c_2	Positive	0,11	1,34	0,2	Positive	0,2
c_3	Positive	0,43	0,77	0,12	Positive	0,12
c_4	Negative	0,89	1,15	0,2	Negative	0,2
c_5	Positive	0,9	2,05	0,16	Positive	0,16
c_6	Positive	0,41	2,04	0,24	Positive	0,24

The DSS will then calculate the SMART and TOPSIS results. The resulting matrix shows different results after computation. Within the SMART method, we document both the aggregated scores for a comprehensive overview and the normalized scores across all criteria to facilitate detailed analysis. In the TOPSIS methodology, we document the aggregated scores, and the distances of the alternatives to the ideal alternative as well as to the negative ideal alternative (nadir). In addition, we record the normalized scores for each criterion. Consequently, the matrix $\mathcal{R}$ is constructed to represent this data, as shown in Table 4. Practitioners have the option to export the result matrix, along with any other matrices, as Excel files for further in-depth analysis.

Table 4. Comparative Results $\mathcal{R}$ using SMART and TOPSIS Methods

(a) Results of the SMART Method

Alternative	Score	c_1	c_2	c_3	c_4	c_5	c_6
Switzerland	81.08	8.00	20.00	0.00	13.08	16.00	24.00
Germany	77.08	7.27	7.97	12.00	17.69	14.33	17.82
France	52.34	6.55	0.00	1.41	20.00	8.63	15.75
Italy	13.84	0.00	3.25	10.59	0.00	0.00	0.00
Austria	52.71	5.09	13.17	4.59	0.77	13.77	15.31

(b) Results of the TOPSIS Method

Alternative	Score	Distance to Ideal	Distance to Nadir	c_1	c_2	c_3	c_4	c_5	c_6
Switzerland	0.86	0.03	0.20	0.13	0.76	0.32	0.43	0.54	0.61
Germany	0.59	0.09	0.13	0.20	0.34	0.57	0.40	0.50	0.48
France	0.39	0.15	0.10	0.26	0.06	0.35	0.39	0.40	0.44
Italy	0.16	0.18	0.03	0.85	0.18	0.54	0.50	0.24	0.12
Austria	0.64	0.07	0.13	0.39	0.52	0.41	0.50	0.49	0.43

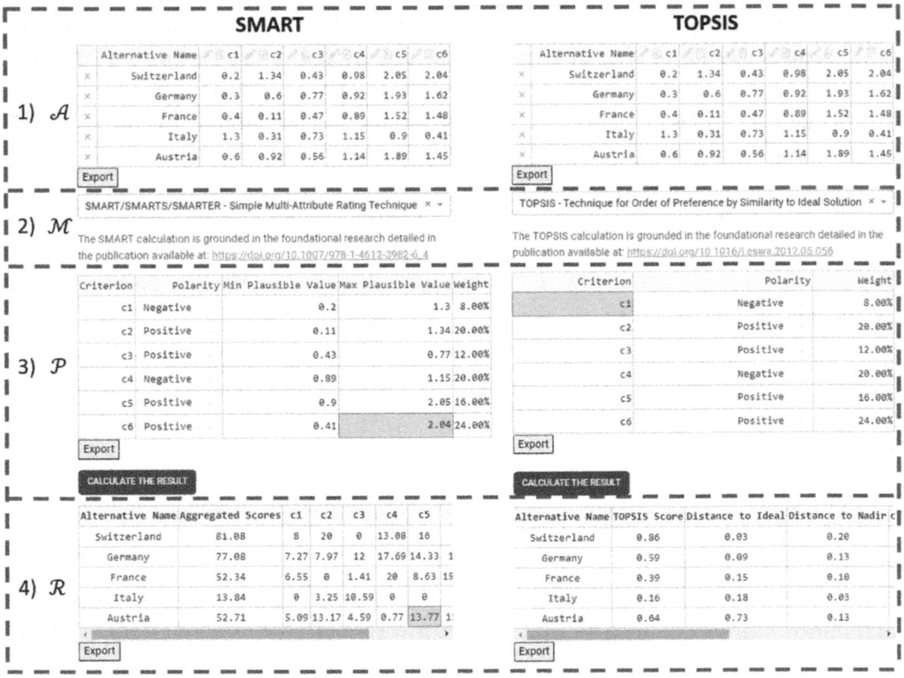

Fig. 4. DSS Workflow with SMART and TOPSIS

We can elaborate how the calculation of SMART and TOPSIS is done in our computational model $\mathcal{F}$ in the web-based DSS, as illustrated in Fig. 3. Practitioners can leverage the MCDA Calculator's linear and reversible workflow to easily adjust parameters or compare results across MCDA methods. By streamlining the calculation process and providing essential functionality in an accessible format, the MCDA Calculator stands out as a practical, time-saving tool in the field of MCDA, filling a critical gap in the current landscape of DSS.

5 Conclusion and Outlook

In this study, we have introduced the MCDA Calculator, a streamlined, web-based DSS specifically designed for facilitating MCDA calculations. This tool is optimized to support the MCDA process by simplifying the workflow and focusing primarily on delivering calculation results and associated parameters. Practitioners are guided through four straightforward steps, from data import to the exportation of MCDA results, making it particularly beneficial for scenarios requiring swift MCDA computations across different methods without the need to switch between various software platforms.

However, it is important to acknowledge that the MCDA Calculator is still in its developmental stages, presenting significant opportunities for enhancement. A key direction for future development involves expanding the range of MCDA methods incorporated within the system. As the MCDA-MSS suggests, there are up to 65 methods (including original MCDA methods and their variants) compatible with our DSS's framework [8]. This indicates a promising direction for extending the calculator's functionality.

While the MCDA Calculator features computational capabilities, the MCDA process encompasses additional aspects such as weighting and sensitivity analysis. Herein lies the potential to evolve the MCDA calculator into a comprehensive, modular DSS. This system would retain the streamlined computational workflow of the MCDA Calculator while integrating it with other modules to handle different aspects of the MCDA process. Such an advancement would not only maintain the efficiency of the MCDA Calculator, but also expand its scope to cover a wider range of MCDA functionalities, providing a holistic and versatile tool for multi-criteria decision analysis.

Acknowledgments. The research published in this article was carried out with the support of the Swiss Federal Office of Energy (SFOE) as part of the SWEET project SURE. The authors bear sole responsibility for the conclusions and the results presented in this publication.

Disclosure of Interests. The authors have no competing interests to declare that are relevant to the content of this article.

References

1. Behzadian, M., Otaghsara, S.K., Yazdani, M., Ignatius, J.: A state-of-the-art survey of topsis applications. Expert Syst. Appl. **39**(17), 13051–13069 (2012)
2. Belton, V., Stewart, T.: Multiple criteria decision analysis: an integrated approach. Springer Science & Business Media (2002)

3. Bigaret, S., Hodgett, R.E., Meyer, P., Mironova, T., Olteanu, A.L.: Supporting the multi-criteria decision aiding process: R and the mcda package. EURO J. Decision Proc. **5**(1–4), 169–194 (2017)
4. Bigaret, S., Meyer, P.: Diviz: an mcda workflow design, execution and sharing tool. Newsletter of the EURO Working Group Multicriteria Aid Decisions **3**(21), 10–13 (2010)
5. Bottero, M., Ferretti, V., Mondini, G.: Constructing multi-attribute value functions for sustainability assessment of urban projects. In: Murgante, B., et al. (eds.) ICCSA 2014. LNCS, vol. 8581, pp. 51–64. Springer, Cham (2014). https://doi.org/10.1007/978-3-319-09150-1_5
6. Brans, J.P., De Smet, Y.: Promethee methods. Multiple criteria decision analysis: state of the art surveys, pp. 187–219 (2016)
7. Chacon-Hurtado, J.C., Scholten, L.: Decisi-o-rama: an open-source python library for multi-attribute value/utility decision analysis. Environm. Model. Softw. **135**, 104890 (2021)
8. Cinelli, M., Kadziński, M., Miebs, G., Gonzalez, M., Słowiński, R.: Recommending multiple criteria decision analysis methods with a new taxonomy-based decision support system. Eur. J. Oper. Res. **302**(2), 633–651 (2022)
9. Cinelli, M., Spada, M., Kim, W., Zhang, Y., Burgherr, P.: Mcda index tool: an interactive software to develop indices and rankings. Environ. Syst. Decis. **41**(1), 82–109 (2021)
10. Dabbas, E.: Interactive Dashboards and Data Apps with Plotly and Dash: Harness the power of a fully fledged frontend web framework in Python–no JavaScript required. Packt Publishing Ltd.(2021)
11. Edwards, W.: How to use multiattribute utility measurement for social decision-making. IEEE Trans. Syst. Man Cybern. **7**(5), 326–340 (1977)
12. Farquhar, P.H.: State of the art-utility assessment methods. Manage. Sci. **30**(11), 1283–1300 (1984)
13. Fossile, D.K., Frej, E.A., da Costa, S.E.G., de Lima, E.P., de Almeida, A.T.: Selecting the most viable renewable energy source for brazilian ports using the fitradeoff method. J. Clean. Prod. **260**, 121107 (2020)
14. Frej, E.A., de Almeida, A.T., Costa, A.P.C.S.: Using data visualization for ranking alternatives with partial information and interactive tradeoff elicitation. Oper. Res. Int. J. **19**, 909–931 (2019)
15. Greco, S., Figueira, J., Ehrgott, M.: Multiple criteria decision analysis, vol. 37. Springer (2016)
16. Haag, F., Aubert, A.H., Lienert, J.: Valuedecisions, a web app to support decisions with conflicting objectives, multiple stakeholders, and uncertainty. Environ. Model. Softw. **150**, 105361 (2022)
17. Huang, H., Lebeau, P., Macharis, C.: The multi-actor multi-criteria analysis (mamca): new software and new visualizations. In: International Conference on Decision Support System Technology, pp. 43–56. Springer (2020)
18. Ishizaka, A., Nemery, P.: Multi-criteria decision analysis: methods and software. John Wiley & Sons (2013)
19. Kaliszewski, I., Podkopaev, D.: Simple additive weighting-a metamodel for multiple criteria decision analysis methods. Expert Syst. Appl. **54**, 155–161 (2016)
20. Mardani, A., Zavadskas, E.K., Govindan, K., Amat Senin, A., Jusoh, A.: Vikor technique: a systematic review of the state of the art literature on methodologies and applications. Sustainability **8**(1), 37 (2016)

21. Mareschal, B., De Smet, Y.: Visual promethee: Developments of the promethee & gaia multicriteria decision aid methods. In: 2009 IEEE International Conference on Industrial Engineering and Engineering Management, pp. 1646–1649. IEEE (2009)

22. Munda, G.: Multicriteria evaluation in a fuzzy environment: The naiade method. Multicriteria Evaluation in a Fuzzy Environment: Theory and Applications in Ecological Economics, pp. 131–148 (1995)

23. Munda, G.: Qualitative reasoning or quantitative aggregation rules for impact assessment of policy options? a multiple criteria framework. Qual. Quant. **56**(5), 3259–3277 (2022)

24. von Nitzsch, R., Tönsfeuerborn, M., Siebert, J.U.: Decision skill training with the ENTSCHEIDUNGSNAVI. In: de Almeida, A.T., Morais, D.C. (eds.) INSID 2020. LNBIP, vol. 405, pp. 15–30. Springer, Cham (2020). https://doi.org/10.1007/978-3-030-64399-7_2

25. Siraj, S., Leonelli, R.C., Keane, J.A., Mikhailov, L.: Priest: a tool to estimate priorities from inconsistent judgments. In: 2013 IEEE International Conference on Systems, Man, and Cybernetics, pp. 44–49. IEEE (2013)

26. Siraj, S., Mikhailov, L., Keane, J.A.: Priest: an interactive decision support tool to estimate priorities from pairwise comparison judgments. Int. Trans. Oper. Res. **22**(2), 217–235 (2015)

27. Siskos, E., Burgherr, P.: Multicriteria decision support for the evaluation of electricity supply resilience: exploration of interacting criteria. Eur. J. Oper. Res. **298**(2), 611–626 (2022)

28. Vaidya, O.S., Kumar, S.: Analytic hierarchy process: an overview of applications. Eur. J. Oper. Res. **169**(1), 1–29 (2006)

29. Valiris, G., Chytas, P., Glykas, M.: Making decisions using the balanced scorecard and the simple multi-attribute rating technique. Perform. Meas. Metrics **6**(3), 159–171 (2005)

30. Wątróbski, J., Bączkiewicz, A., Sałabun, W.: pyrepo-mcda-reference objects based mcda software package. SoftwareX **19**, 101107 (2022)

Research on Cost Estimation of Launch Vehicle Based on Grey Neural Network

Zihui Liu, Bingfeng Ge$^{(\boxtimes)}$, Yuming Huang, Zeqiang Hou, Wanying Wei, and Jichao Li

College of Systems Engineering, National University of Defense Technology, Changsha, China
{bingfengge,huangyuming14,houzeqiang16,weiwanying}@nudt.edu.cn

Abstract. A cost estimation method for launch vehicles is proposed combining the concepts of machine learning, aims to provide assistance in strategic decision-making processes pertaining to satellite launch activities. First, the characteristics of existing methods for estimating the cost of launch vehicles are analyzed, and draws out the machine learning methods based on the characteristics of the current development of launch vehicles in China. Next, a model algorithm based on a dynamic neural network and grey relational analysis is introduced. This algorithm simplifies the network structure by iteratively eliminating low correlation coefficient nodes, effectively addressing the issue of overfitting in small sample data. Finally, the proposed method is validated through a case study about prediction of the Long March series launch vehicle, demonstrating its feasibility and effectiveness.

Keywords: Launch vehicle · Cost estimation · Grey relational · Neural network

1 Introduction

The development of launch vehicle systems is complex, challenging, and time-consuming, with cost control being a crucial factor in their success. China's launch vehicle development needs to progress from technological breakthroughs to key capability improvements and life-cycle cost control. However, China started its research on launch vehicle cost estimation relatively late, resulting in an imperfect cost analysis system [15]. The ability to collect, sort, and analyze cost data is insufficient, leading to subjective tendencies in cost analysis and a lack of scientific basis in space project demonstrations. Currently, most domestic scholars focus on the issue of small sample sizes and limited information when it comes to cost estimation for space projects. The grey system theory, which is an effective method for predicting small sample data, heavily depends on parameters and may not be applicable in the era of big data [2]. Hence, exploring a cost estimation method for launch vehicles that can handle small sample sizes is strategically significant.

S. P. Duarte et al. (Eds.): ICDSST 2024, LNBIP 506, pp. 46–57, 2024.
https://doi.org/10.1007/978-3-031-59376-5_4

Currently, launch vehicle cost estimation research and implementation primarily focus on two approaches: 1) The "component-whole" hierarchical estimation method, which relies on expert judgment and experience. This method breaks down the rocket cost into various components and estimates each component based on expert knowledge. The estimates are then aggregated to determine the overall cost; 2) The grey system theory-based approach, which involves establishing a mathematical model using limited and incomplete information. This method enables analysis and prediction of the rocket cost structure, considering uncertain factors. Common methods in this approach include data series correlation analysis and data smoothing techniques [13].

Neural networks are intricate systems comprising interconnected simple neurons that leverage nonlinear mapping to represent the implicit relationship between input and output data in samples through learning [4]. Due to their robust self-learning capabilities and intelligent control functions, neural network systems find extensive applications in nonlinear learning control [10]. In handling the challenges posed by incomplete and uncertain data within the domain of large space equipment, the neural network's strong fault tolerance enables it to adeptly navigate these complex scenarios [3].

Building on the aforementioned information, this paper proposes the application of the grey neural network modeling method for launch vehicle cost estimation, integrating the principles of the grey system theory and the characteristics of a neural network model. By combining the grey relational model and neural network model, the proposed approach combines adaptive learning and nonlinear dynamic optimization capabilities. This integration allows for effective handling of nonlinear fuzzy problems, resulting in high prediction accuracy, good error control, and a reasonable demand for sample data.

The remainder of this article is laid out as follows. In Sect. 2, the relevant theory of grey relational model and Back-Propagation (BP) neural network model are reviewed. Section 3 proposes a grey neural network model for the cost estimation of launch vehicles. In Sect. 4, an illustrative example is presented to showcase the practical application and interpretation of the aforementioned approach. Finally, the paper is concluded with the main conclusions in Sect. 5.

2 Preliminaries

2.1 Grey Relational Model

In systems characterized by the presence of vague, unclear, and partially known information, they are often classified as grey systems [11]. Grey relational model is a tool of grey system theory for analyzing the relation ship between a reference series and other series. The grey relational grade serves as an analytical instrument for the assessment and quantification of interactions among system variables and their correlation. The fundamental concept underlying this methodology is to assess the level of correlation between discrete data series based on their geometric similarity [16]. In comparison to conventional techniques such as regression correlation analysis and others, grey relational analysis offers enhanced overall analytical capabilities [7,11,16].

The grey relational grade is represented as a value within the range of 0 to 1. The magnitude of the grey relational grade is instrumental in identifying the principal independent variables that significantly influence the dependent variables. Utilizing variables identified through grey relational analysis for modeling and analysis typically results in improved model fitting performance.

The steps of grey relational analysis are as follows:

Step 1: Determine the reference series and comparison series;

Reference series reflects the behavior characteristics of the system, represented as $x_0(k)$, where $i = 1, 2, \cdots, n$. Comparative series is a series of factors that affect the behavior of a system, represented as $x_i(k)$, where $k = 1, 2, \cdots, n$.

Step 2: Nondimensionalize;

When conducting grey relational degree analysis, it is generally necessary to perform dimensionless data processing since the data in each factor column in the system may have different dimensions. There are two main methods [8]:

$$x_i(k) = \frac{x_i(k)}{x_i(1)} \qquad (1)$$

and

$$x_i(k) = \frac{x_i(k)}{\bar{x}_i}, \qquad (2)$$

where Formula (1) and (2) represent initializing and averaging, respectively.

Step 3: Calculate grey relational coefficient;

The grey relational coefficient can be calculated by the following formula [5]:

$$\xi_{0i}(k) = \frac{\Delta(\min) + \rho\Delta(\max)}{\Delta_{0i}(k) + \rho\Delta(\max)}, \qquad (3)$$

where $\rho \in (0, 1]$, represents the resolution coefficient, usually 0.5, and

$$\Delta_{0i}(k) = |x_0(k) - x_i(k)|, \qquad (4)$$

represents the absolute value of the difference between the two series,

$$\Delta(\min) = \min_i \min_k (\Delta_{0i}), \qquad (5)$$

$$\Delta(\max) = \max_i \max_k (\Delta_{0i}), \qquad (6)$$

are the minimal and maximal proximity, respectively.

Step 4: Calculate grey relational grade;

The grey relational grade can be calculated by the following formula [1,5,9]:

$$r_{0i} = \sum_{k=1}^{n} \omega(k)\xi_{0i}(k), \tag{7}$$

where $\omega(k)$ are weights such that $0 \leqslant \omega(k) \leqslant 1$ and $\sum_{k=1}^{n}\omega(k) = 1$. For convenience, we simply take $\omega(k) = \frac{1}{n}$ for all k.

Step 5: Relational ranking.

If grey relational grade $r_{01} < r_{02}$, it indicates that reference series $x_0(k)$ is more similar to comparison series $x_2(k)$.

2.2 BP Neural Network Model

BP neural network, also known as the back propagation network, is an interdisciplinary field that encompasses artificial intelligence, neurology, cognitive science, computer science, and other related disciplines [18]. It models the input and output relationships by simulating the human brain, enabling the simulation of highly complex relationships. The BP neural network exhibits strong adaptive, self-organizing, nonlinear dynamic processing capabilities, as well as real-time learning abilities [19].

The network topology structure of BP neural network is depicted in Fig. 1. It consists of an input layer, a hidden layer, and an output layer. Neurons within each layer are fully connected, whereas neurons within the same layer do not have connections [17–19]. The main idea of BP algorithm is the learning process into signal forward propagation and error back propagation in two stages.

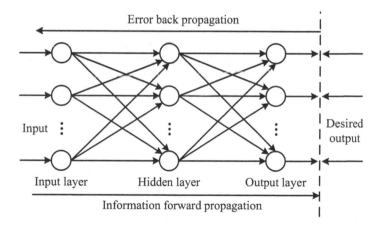

Fig. 1. BP neural network model

The steps of BP neural network are as follows:

Step 1: Initializing the network;

Step 2: Calculate the hidden layer output;

The output I_j can be calculated by the following formula [19]:

$$I_j = f(\sum \lambda_{ij} Y_i - \theta_j), \tag{8}$$

where f is the activation function, Y_i is the input of input layer, λ_{ij} represents the neuron connection weight between input layer and hidden layer, and θ_i is the hidden layer neuron threshold.

Step 3: Calculate the hidden layer output;

The output O_j can be calculated by the following formula [19]:

$$O_j = g(\sum \mu_{ij} I_i - \theta_j'), \tag{9}$$

where g is the activation function, I_j is the input of input layer, μ_{ij} represents the neuron connection weight between hidden layer and output layer, θ_j' is the output layer neuron threshold, and O_j is the output of output layer.

Step 4: Update neuron connection weight and neuron threshold by error calculation;

The error function can be expressed as [14]:

$$E = \sum (d_j - O_j)^2, \tag{10}$$

where d_j represents the desired output. The traditional BP neural network model employs the gradient descent method for reverse updating.

Step 5: Repeat the above steps until reaching the required error range.

3   Grey Neural Network Model

The approximation ability of a neural network is improved with an increase in the number of hidden layer neurons. However, it is important to consider the learning speed of neural networks as having too many hidden layer neurons can lead to slow optimization speed [12]. In practical applications, the number of hidden layer neurons has often been determined using the empirical formula:

$$\varphi = \sqrt{b + c} + \eta, \tag{11}$$

where $\eta \in [1, 10]$, b and c represent the number of network input and output neurons, respectively.

This Section proposes a combination of the neural network with the grey relational analysis. When the network learning meets the error requirement, the output sequence of the hidden layer neurons is analyzed in relation to the network's expected output [5]. The size of the grey relational grade indicates the ability of the hidden layer neurons outputs to change with the network output values. A smaller grey relational grade signifies a lesser influence of the neurons on the network output, allowing for the deletion of certain hidden layer neurons to achieve the desired pruning effect [9].

As shown in Fig. 2, the specific steps are as follows:

Step 1: Normalization;

Import the data and utilize the normalization function to process both the input and output data falls within the range [-1, 1].

Step 2: Initializing the network;

Step 3: Training BP neural network;

In the construction of the BP neural network, certain functions are applied, such as activation functions for the hidden and output layers, as well as the network training function. These functions are set and trained simultaneously during the modeling process.

Step 4: Grey relational analysis to hidden layer neurons; The neuron grey relational coefficient can be calculated by the following formula:

$$\zeta(j) = \frac{\Delta(\min) + \alpha\Delta(\max)}{\Delta(j) + \alpha\Delta(\max)}, \tag{12}$$

where $\alpha \in (0, 1]$, represents the resolution coefficient, usually 0.5, and

$$\Delta(j) = |O_j - d_j|, \tag{13}$$

represents the absolute value of the difference between the two series,

$$\Delta(\min) = \min\min(\Delta(j)), \tag{14}$$

$$\Delta(\max) = \max\max(\Delta(j)), \tag{15}$$

are the minimal and maximal proximity, respectively.

The neuron grey relational grade can be calculated by the following formula:

$$\delta = \frac{1}{m}\sum_{j=1}^{m}\zeta(j), \tag{16}$$

Step 5: Optimize the network structure;

Remove neurons with low grey relational grade.

Step 6: Whether all neuron grey relational grades meet the threshold. If not, return to *Step 2*;

Step 7: Prediction analysis based on trained model.

4 Illustrative Example

4.1 Data Obtainment and Processing

In the current research on launch vehicle cost estimation, one often encounters challenges such as limited data availability and inadequate information [6]. In this Section, reliable information was gathered by sourcing open data from official public platforms, including online news reports, space enthusiasts networks, the SpaceX official website, and the China Aerospace Science and Technology

Corporation official website[1]. The selected sources ensure a high level of credibility.

The cost manual introduced by NASA demonstrates significant capabilities in data collection, analysis, and prediction. This paper summarizes and identifies seven key parameters for launch vehicle cost estimation by referencing the process of parametric cost estimation outlined in the NASA cost manual.

These parameters include vehicle length (m), maximum diameter of the core stage (m), take-off mass (t), take-off thrust (kN), stage number, carrying capacity (t), and launch cost (10m$). The dataset primarily focuses on typical and advanced rockets associated with the United States and Europe. It specifically comprises renowned launch vehicles such as the Hercules series, Pegasus series, Taurus series, Delta series, Saturn series, Cosmos series, Falcon series, and other American series. This dataset offers broad coverage and distinct characteristics.

To ensure the validity of the data, several steps were taken. Firstly, the accuracy of the data were checked, revealing issues such as fuzzy information, interval scales, and noisy nature of the data. Secondly, a thorough examination was conducted to verify whether the data truly reflected the objective reality. This included checking for logical consistency, assessing if the content aligned with reality, and identifying any potential contradictions between items or figures.

In view of the above problems, through data preprocessing techniques such as filling in default values, smoothing noisy data, identifying and removing outliers, and resolving inconsistencies, a total of 54 valid data points were obtained.

4.2   Model Fitting

Based on the preprocessed dataset, a grey neural network model is constructed in MATLAB using the algorithm principles mentioned. The model employs a three-layer network topology known for its strong universality. In this model, the input layer consists of 6 neurons corresponding to the 6 key parameters, while the output layer has 1 neuron representing the estimated launch cost. To address issues like data overfitting, the number of neurons in the hidden layer was initially set to 10. It was then iteratively adjusted using grey relational analysis to meet the importance threshold.

For the BP neural network, the following parameter settings were applied: a training rate of 0.05, a target error accuracy of 1×10^{-6}, a maximum of 1000 iterations during the cyclic training process, a tansig activation function for the hidden layer, a purelin activation function for the output layer, and the default trainlm network training function. The model was trained and fitted using 49 data points, while 5 data points corresponding to different types of rockets were used for testing. The specifics of the data can be found in Table 1.

---

[1] Data source URL:

1. http://www.spaceflightfans.cn.
2. https://www.spacex.com.
3. http://www.spacechina.com.
4. https://www.heavens-above.com.

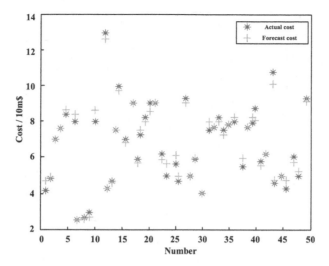

Fig. 2. Training set fitting effect

Table 1. Data type and training division

		Number	Amount
Training	Hercules	1–6	6
	Pegasus	7–9	3
	Saturn	10–11	2
	Delta	12–17	6
set	Cosmos	18–21	4
	Falcon 9	22–42	21
	Others	43–49	6
Test set		50–54	5

Through repeated training tests, it has been observed that when the number of neurons in the hidden layer converges to a range of 3–5, the issue of overfitting in the training set is mitigated. This results in a satisfactory overall fitting effect, as illustrated in Fig. 2.

The comparison of prediction results in Fig. 3 demonstrates that, for the limited small-sample dataset used in this study, the average cost estimation error of the well-trained model during prediction is below 10 million dollars. This performance essentially fulfills the prediction expectations and establishes a solid foundation for future applied research.

4.3   Prediction Analysis of Long March Series Launch Vehicle

In the current dynamic and rapidly evolving international landscape, with increasing competition for space resources, it is anticipated that the Long March

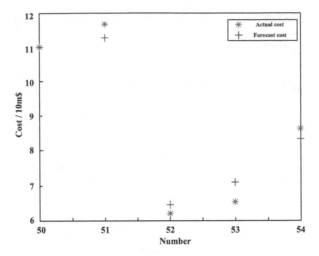

Fig. 3. Test set prediction effect

series of rockets will undergo faster upgrades and iterations, leading to a higher launch frequency. Additionally, with the introduction of the United States' "Starlink" program, if China intends to develop its own similar initiative, the Long March series of rockets will play a crucial role and hold a more stable strategic position. This Section seeks to obtain a reliable cost estimation model by training data from various types of foreign rockets. The aim is to predict the cost development of the existing Long March rockets in China.

The data presented in Table 2 represents the key indicators of several typical Long March carrier rockets in China. This data was collected from reliable sources, including the official website of China Aerospace Science and Technology Corporation and the official website of the National Aeronautics and Space Administration[2]. As stated in 4.1, the seven key parameters considered are vehicle length (m), maximum diameter of the core (m), take-off mass (t), take-off thrust (kN), stage number, carrying capacity (t), and launch cost (10 m$).

Regarding the launch costs, experts have noted that the launch cost of the Long March 4 carrier rocket can be estimated between 3.75×10m$ and 4.25×10m$. For this paper, the median value of 4×10m$ is adopted as the launch cost of the Long March 4 carrier rocket. According to publicly available data on the official website of the China Academy of Launch Vehicle, the launch cost per kilogram is approximately 30,000 dollars. Based on the payload capacity, the launch cost of the Long March 11 carrier rocket can be calculated to be approximately 2.1×10m$. Upon analyzing the known data in Table 2, a preliminary

---

[2] Data source URL:

1. http://www.spacechina.com.
2. https://www.cnsa.gov.cn.

Table 2. Long March series launch vehicle data set

Type	Vehicle length (m)	Maximum diameter of the core (m)	Take-off mass (t)	Take-off thrust (kN)	Stage number	Carrying capacity (t)	Launch cost (10m$)
Long March 2D	33.667	3.35	237	2961	2	3.1	3.6
Long March 3B	54.84	3.35	426	5923.2	3	2.6	4.8
Long March 4B	45.576	3.35	248.47	2971	3	2.2	4
Long March 5	56.97	5	851.8	10524	3	25	10
Long March 7	53.075	3.35	597	7203	2	12	6
Long March 8	50.3	3.35	356	4704	2	7.6	5.5
Long March 11	20.8	2	57.6	1176	4	0.7	2.1

observation reveals that the launch cost of the launch vehicle exhibits a positive correlation with each parameter in the table, and the magnitude of the correlation remains stable. By searching for data on the internet and combining it with official launch cost data, the launch costs of other types of launch vehicles can be obtained. Finally, based on information from network platforms and calculations, the launch costs of the Long March 2D carrier rocket, the Long March 3B carrier rocket, the Long March 5 carrier rocket, the Long March 7 carrier rocket, and the Long March 8 carrier rocket are estimated to be 3.6×10m$, 4.8×10m$, 10×10m$, 6×10m$, and 5.5×10m$, respectively.

According to the model trained in Sect. 3, the launch cost of China's Long March carrier rocket is predicted, and the stable and satisfactory forecast data is obtained, as shown in Fig. 4.

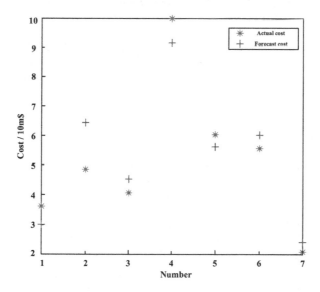

Fig. 4. Forecast cost of Long March launch vehicles

The predicted launch cost is found to have a small difference compared to the calculated launch cost based on expert experience, with the exception of the

Long March 3B carrier rocket, which exhibits a significant difference from the predicted value. Through analysis, it is determined that occasional substantial differences between forecast and actual data are normal. The launch cost of a carrier rocket is not solely determined by specific capability indices but is also influenced to some extent by factors such as political, economic, military, public welfare requirements, and scientific research significance. The impact of these factors varies depending on the specific launch mission and domestic and foreign environmental factors.

5   Conclusion

This paper proposes an innovative approach to equipment life cycle management. This approach combines the principles of big data thinking and employs a grey model to obtain a dynamic BP neural network model through grey relational analysis. The paper applies this method to cost estimation during the demonstration stage of equipment life cycle management in the Long March series launch vehicle. The model is then tested and analyzed using real data cases. The results of the analysis demonstrate that the proposed model, when applied to appropriate data, offers several advantages over traditional cost estimation methods. These advantages include strong adaptability to different situations, high utilization of information, and accurate cost estimation. The findings of the research provide a theoretical foundation for the demonstration and decision-making of new launch vehicle projects.

Acknowledgement. This work was supported in part by the National Natural Science Foundation of China (NSFC) under Grants (71971213, and 72301288), and by the General Project of Postgraduate Scientific Research Innovation Project of Hunan Province (Grant No. CX20230086).

References

1. Chu, J., Xiao, X.: Benefits evaluation of the northeast passage based on grey relational degree of discrete z-numbers. Inf. Sci. **626**, 607–625 (2023)
2. Deng, J., et al.: Introduction to grey system theory. J. Grey Syst. **1**(1), 1–24 (1989)
3. Elbrächter, D., Perekrestenko, D., Grohs, P., Bölcskei, H.: Deep neural network approximation theory. IEEE Trans. Inf. Theory **67**(5), 2581–2623 (2021)
4. Hansun, S., Wicaksana, A., Khaliq, A.Q.: Multivariate cryptocurrency prediction: comparative analysis of three recurrent neural networks approaches. J. Big Data **9**(1), 1–15 (2022)
5. Hu, Y.C.: Constructing grey prediction models using grey relational analysis and neural networks for magnesium material demand forecasting. Appl. Soft Comput. **93**, 106398 (2020)
6. Jo, B.U., Ahn, J.: Optimal staging of reusable launch vehicles for minimum life cycle cost. Aerosp. Sci. Technol. **127**, 107703 (2022)
7. Kuo, T.: A review of some modified grey relational analysis models. J. Grey Syst. **29**(3), 70–78 (2017)

8. Liu, S.: Negative grey relational model and measurement of the reverse incentive effect of fields medal. Grey Syst. Theory Appl. **13**(1), 1–13 (2023)

9. Manikandan, N., Raju, R., Palanisamy, D., Binoj, J.: Optimisation of spark erosion machining process parameters using hybrid grey relational analysis and artificial neural network model. Int. J. Mach. Mach. Mater. **22**(1), 1–23 (2020)

10. McCulloch, W.S., Pitts, W.: A logical calculus of the ideas immanent in nervous activity. Bull. Math. Biophys. **5**, 115–133 (1943)

11. Prakash, S., Agrawal, A., Singh, R., Singh, R.K., Zindani, D.: A decade of grey systems: theory and application-bibliometric overview and future research directions. Grey Syst. Theory Appl. **13**(1), 14–33 (2023)

12. Radhakrishnan, A., Belkin, M., Uhler, C.: Wide and deep neural networks achieve consistency for classification. Proc. Natl. Acad. Sci. **120**(14), e2208779120 (2023)

13. Schwabe, O., Shehab, E., Erkoyuncu, J.: Uncertainty quantification metrics for whole product life cycle cost estimates in aerospace innovation. Prog. Aerosp. Sci. **77**, 1–24 (2015)

14. Song, S., Xiong, X., Wu, X., Xue, Z.: Modeling the SOFC by BP neural network algorithm. Int. J. Hydrogen Energy **46**(38), 20065–20077 (2021)

15. Uhalley, S., Jr.: China's aerospace prowess today and tomorrow. Am. J. Chin. Stud. **25**(1), 63–79 (2018)

16. Wang, F.: Research on the model and application progress based on grey relational analysis theory. Adv. Educ. Technol. Psychol. **5**(2), 30–35 (2021)

17. Wu, W., Wang, J., Cheng, M., Li, Z.: Convergence analysis of online gradient method for BP neural networks. Neural Netw. **24**(1), 91–98 (2011)

18. Zhang, X., Sun, X., Sun, W., Xu, T., Wang, P., Jha, S.K.: Deformation expression of soft tissue based on BP neural network. Intell. Autom. Soft Comput. **32**(2), 1041–1053 (2022)

19. Zhang, Y., Dong, D., Sha, J.: Traffic track dynamic data analysis based on BP neural network model. In: 2023 3rd International Conference on Neural Networks, Information and Communication Engineering (NNICE), pp. 1–4. IEEE (2023)

A Decision Support Tool for Paratransit Systems Planning

Vitor Oliveira[1]([envelope]), Thiago Sobral[2][iD], José Telhada[3][iD],
and Maria do Sameiro Carvalho[3][iD]

[1] University of Minho, Braga, Portugal
engvitor@gmail.com
[2] Faculty of Engineering of the University of Porto, Porto, Portugal
thiago.sobral@fe.up.pt
[3] Department of Production and Systems Engineering, University of Minho, Braga,
Portugal
{telhada,sameiro}@dps.uminho.pt

Abstract. Paratransit systems are designed to cater to individuals with reduced mobility, and have played a pivotal role in providing essential mobility and accessibility for those who often encounter challenges with conventional public transport. These systems rely on flexible transport, and are characterised by their high configurability and uncertainty stemming from factors such as low demand, complexity, and the specific mobility needs of the targeted group. Unfortunately, some of these systems have encountered failures due to structural and parameterisation errors.

This paper proposes a Decision Support System (DSS) to support the strategic and tactical decisions of conception and design of paratransit systems, as well as to support operational management. This system aims to integrate the interests of different stakeholders during the decision-making process in order to obtain more robust solutions.

Particular focus is given to a segment of the DSS that interfaces with operational management and simulation components. This integration facilitates the assessment and comparison of alternative scenarios, utilizing diverse criteria to achieve the most suitable parameterisation and comprehend the associated risks tied to specific decisions. The tool provides assistance across various decision-making scenarios, and within this context, we will scrutinize its efficacy in identifying and comprehending the impacts of varying time window sizes on the systems' performance.

The outcomes of these analyses underscore the significance of contemplating diverse parameters in decisions related to mobility. The tool provides valuable insights, enabling better alignment with genuine needs, and ensuring that devised solutions align with user preferences.

Keywords: Decision Support Tool · Paratransit systems · Demand responsive transport · Persons with Reduced Mobility

S. P. Duarte et al. (Eds.): ICDSST 2024, LNBIP 506, pp. 58–69, 2024.
https://doi.org/10.1007/978-3-031-59376-5_5

1   Introduction

Defining a strategy is a fundamental aspect of every organisation, regardless of whether it is public or private, small or large in scale. However, formulating a strategy requires decision-making regarding the actions required within the organisation to achieve medium and long-term objectives. For a specific decision to be supported, decision-makers must possess a wealth of information, highlighting utility and necessity.

The implementation of an innovative transport service aimed at a specific public with low demand requires greater flexibility, while at the same time having the ability to minimize service costs [3,4,7,12,20]. In many cases, the solution involves the implementation of agile services capable of meeting users' needs. However, caution is needed when implementing flexible services such as Demand-responsive transport (DRT), as there are examples of promising DRT schemes that have failed [13].

The use of Business Intelligence (BI) tools allows to improve the management and optimisation of operations in the organisations, providing the means for data-based decisions and aligned with the strategy. A decision support system, combined with reliable data sources, facilitates the decision-making process [14]. With the increase in demand and in an attempt to reduce costs in on-demand transport systems, decision support and planning models for new transport systems have emerged [8].

Nonetheless, creating these models can be challenging due to the high level of complexity and the specificities inherent to paratransit systems. The existence of various system types, involving different decision makers with different objectives increases the complexity of the decision-making process, and some decisions may overlook the specific characteristics of the area. The tool proposed in this paper addresses this challenge, providing more comprehensive and easy-to-understand knowledge about the process.

To support decision-makers and make the process more efficient, it would be beneficial to use a tool that could help define parameters and analyse results. The objective of the proposed model to ensure that decision-makers focus on the important aspects of decisions, without getting lost in the technical details of the process of collecting and processing operational data, which normally involves a large amount of information. The development of the tool is oriented towards different decision makers, providing visualisations of solutions, allowing the analysis and experimentation of multiple configurations. Furthermore, the tool can adjust parameters and try different scenarios to obtain different perspectives on the problem, finding the final solution that reflects the needs of people with reduced mobility. Overall, the tool aims to make the decision-making process more accessible and efficient, providing more informed and effective decisions.

The Decision Support System (DSS) can assist decision makers on several fronts, one of which is related to defining the time windows to be used during planning. Determining this parameter is crucial for passenger satisfaction, as they expect the service to be carried out at the indicated times. However, this choice impacts several aspects of the system, such as flexibility, the size and number of routes required, costs, resources, etc. The case study focuses especially on this point, seeking to exemplify how the DSS will contribute to assisting decision-makers in making decisions and what the consequences of this choice will be, in addition to helping to understand how the trend is evolving when making a variation.

The remaining sections of the document are structured as follows. Section 2 provides an overview of the paratransit system and outlines how the decision support system can aid in decision-making. Section 3 encompasses the general architecture of the tool. Section 4 reports on an illustrative case study based on simulation data from a paratransit system. Lastly, Sect. 5 offers a succinct conclusion, emphasizing the potential use of this tool in enhancing decision-making, and discusses possible directions for future work.

2   Background

People with reduced mobility do not see conventional public transport (bus/train) as a comfortable and safe means of travel, and encounter many barriers in its use [11,17]. These barriers have been progressively eliminated due to changes in current practice, due to regulation, although they do not cease to exist, and it is mainly necessary to understand them. There is a gap in the knowledge about the connection between public transport and people with disabilities [19], as well as people with cognitive disabilities [15].

The elderly and people with disabilities still have difficulty using public transport, despite the improvements implemented [9,18]. The barriers are such that people choose not to travel as a way of not feeling discriminated against, humiliated due to their difficulties, also leading to a reduction in self-confidence, impotence and feelings of inferiority [16].

Some countries have already implemented alternative transport systems, but not all, successfully due to strategic errors in implementation, and in the choice of resources or configuration. Furthermore, the market is in an expansion phase and is experiencing an increase in the supply of door-to-door services [6].

The implementation of an innovative transport service aimed at a specific public and low demand requires greater flexibility, while also seeking to minimize service costs [3,7,20]. In many cases, the solution involves implementing solutions that use more agile transport with the ability to respond to users' needs.

The used architecture comprises advanced data analysis with the aim of serving the requirements of various types of users/decision makers, not only internal but also external to the organisation. Acting as a basis for data analysis tools with the possibility of multiplicity of information analysis from different angles, perspectives and forms.

The tool is based on a set of theories, methodologies, processing architectures that can transform raw data into continuous and systematic information [1,10] through the organised structure and for the management of large amounts of data [2] in order to identify and develop new opportunities for more effective strategy implementation [10] and improvements, due to the transformation of data into information [2] and the production of knowledge and insights approach to the market [1], timely availability [5], improving logistics and sales efficiency, optimizing marketing and minimizing risks.

The search for trends and relationships can improve operational efficiency, monitoring, tactical definition, as well as strategic management and decision-making support, providing competitive advantages. The exploration of BI technologies applied to the paratransit system contributes to supporting decision-making on parameters, aiming to improve the quality of services and reduce the costs of public transport for passengers with reduced mobility in urban areas, mainly in the design of an organisational structure and operational management.

The focus of this work is to study a decision support system for the implementation phase to support operational management, considering a set of parameters that can influence transport flexibility. Development is not limited to route planning, it also focuses on operational management and simulation of the entire system based on scenarios, in order to develop an intelligent management system.

3   General Architecture

Despite the effectiveness of route planning algorithms and the greater computational capacity to update them, on-demand transport systems still do not offer sufficient guarantees for successful implementation. These systems require a solid structure and configuration that meets the specific needs of the area and demand. The setup is complex and requires comprehensive understanding, encompassing multiple stakeholders with conflicting interests, such as opening hours or areas each operator can cover, as well as the flexibility to adjust routes.

The Decision Support System (DSS) architecture is designed primarily to support the decision-making process about what should be the best configuration to be applied in a given area and demand. This architecture requires a module responsible for generating input data, consisting of an operational management application and a simulator. The DSS collects data, which is transformed to obtain a set of key performance indicators (KPIs) and made available to decision makers in different formats, according to their needs. This tool can significantly improve the speed, efficiency and effectiveness of decisions, by visualizing relevant information, configuring the necessary values and comparing KPIs between different scenarios. Figure 1 is a visual representation of the key elements.

The first part is responsible for generating the input data for the DSS. These can come from real data or simulations, using an operational management tool and a simulator, as in the case presented. The main objectives of the operational management tool are recording mobility requests, planning routes and communicating planning results. The simulator reproduces the events corresponding to mobility requests, the movement of vehicles, the behavior of drivers and passengers, according to the instructions received by the operational management tool.

To generate data, it is necessary to provide a set of input data that allows the parameterisation of the application and the simulator. The operational

Fig. 1. General architecture of the proposed model

management tool must contain information about the network (stops, connections between stops and their characteristics, such as distance, weather forecast throughout the day, etc.), the types of services to be used (fixed, flexible or mixed, in terms of sequence of stops or crossing times), times for performing services and accepting new services, including those that occur after planning, information about vehicles and their characteristics, including special requirements and temporal availability.

The simulator performs three essential tasks: generating mobility requests, data on vehicle movement and data on customer behavior. This is done based on discrete events and in chronological order. An event represents an action that someone or something must take at a certain time.

To generate mobility requests, data is needed on the probability of a stop generating a request, including special characteristics (e.g. wheelchair), the formula to calculate the service start time, the origin-destination matrix with the probability of movement from one stop to another, the average number of orders to be generated and the standard to be applied.

The movement of vehicles takes into account the sequence of stops resulting from planning, calculating the travel time between stops based on the relationship between distance and speed. The time required for stops for passenger entry or exit or increased by new requests is also calculated. This value is determined by a historical pattern at different times and days of the week, seeking to reproduce normal movement, taking into account the most appropriate speed for the customers to be transported, possible congestion, works, accidents, weather conditions, etc.

Data on customer behavior is summarised in three moments: arrival at stops, entry and exit of vehicles. Arrival at the stop is calculated based on the expected time defined during planning, adding a random value to simulate passenger arrivals earlier than expected (growing quadratically) and later than expected (approaching a negative exponential form). The duration of the transition is equal, with exits occurring before entries. To determine this value, the characteristics of the passenger and the number of passengers inside the vehicle are considered.

The final results consist of a set of data on mobility services and their characteristics, as well as planning results, the times these services are carried out and also the arrival times of passengers at stops.

The ETL process represents the second part of the DSS architecture. The system must include data extraction, transformation and storage. Data may be stored and/or produced by different systems to be used on a daily basis, and are therefore frequently modified or deleted, which limits their access and historical reconstruction. Thus, an important step is the data extraction process, which can be conditioned by several considerations, including the period and frequency with which the data must be collected, the location and cadence of access to it, its quality and quantity, between others.

Data transformation is a step where the original data is cleaned, processed, standardised, organised and where the values of performance indicators are calculated. The last step is to store the data in a robust structure that allows quick access to information whenever necessary.

The third step of the architecture corresponds to data analysis and reporting capabilities, which allow relevant insights to be obtained for decision makers. With the available data, it is possible to identify past trends, patterns and performance metrics, developing a descriptive analysis of the different states and areas of operations. This may include statistical techniques, data mining, machine learning, simulations, among others. We seek to understand how certain events occurred, work on the causes of inefficiency and act proactively to anticipate needs and problems.

The final part of the DSS architecture is related to the user interface (UI), which must be intuitive. The UI mainly aims to display data according to the specificity of the information and the needs of decision makers, creating personalised reports. The practical visualisation of this part is through simplified reports based on graphs, diagrams, tables, maps and other visual representations of data and analysis, in real time or periodically. Visualisation through control panels helps in monitoring daily activities, using interactive panels. Reports help to understand how operations are evolving, helping to adjust strategies as necessary and helping to manage resources and define the correct configuration.

The integration of simulation into the DSS for the paratransit system allows for more informed and proactive decision-making, helping to anticipate present and future scenarios, identify opportunities for improvement and mitigate potential risks. With integration, it is possible to simulate the impact of different policies, typologies and rules, in addition to carrying out sensitivity analyzes to understand how changes in key variables, such as time windows, service rates, waiting time, among others, affect the operational and financial results. Strategy validation allows you to analyze growth strategies, such as expansion into new areas or the introduction and combination of new typologies, to assess their viability and the impact the system will have on the community.

4 Application Example

Here we intend to analyze how the definition of storm windows will influence the time difference between the desired time (time indicated by the user) and the predicted time (programmed), this difference will reflect the satisfaction that users will have in relation to the system. The time window corresponds to the time interval in which the service can be performed. The desired time is the reference to create this time interval, with the window being divided into two parts, one before and the other after the desired time, and these values will be parameterised.

The larger the time window, the more flexible the system becomes, which means that there are greater combinations of service sequences and, therefore, cost minimisation. By creating several scenarios, the sensitivity of the system in relation to the size of the temporal windows and their internal subdivision can be analyzed.

The scenarios are built based on a virtual network made up of 307 stopping points, distributed non-uniformly across 12 areas, providing greater relevance to the areas and stops. Furthermore, reasons for travel, such as health, school, leisure and others, were also considered. An origin-destination matrix was established between the areas. Between adjacent stops, a distance and a set of duration's were defined to indicate the average travel time during different periods of the day.

Data generation results from the interaction between the operational management tool and the simulator. The simulator is responsible for generating the orders and sending them. Requests are generated randomly taking into account the origin destination matrix of the areas, the weight of the stops and the reasons. The time of the request is generated randomly according to a formula that allows you to obtain a histogram similar to that of regular public transport.

The operational management tool is configured with a typology to respond to a door-to-door transport system without any restrictions between stops and vehicles. Route planning follows Xang's heuristics [21], with adaptations to prioritize requests involving people with wheelchairs or similar situations. The choice of this heuristic is due to the speed of obtaining a solution in a short period of time. Additionally, a post-optimizer was incorporated that performs random changes in the position of orders.

4.1   Creation of Scenarios

The objective is to establish the ideal size of time windows and their distribution during planning, aiming to minimize costs and time discrepancy in relation to the desired time, which, in turn, would increase user satisfaction.

In each simulated scenario, a time interval corresponding to one year is adopted, during which the stability of the solutions is achieved. To create a new scenario, we start from a base scenario, copy the data and adjust the parameters under analysis.

To understand how the values presented can influence the system, 59 scenarios were simulated, with 3 different time windows. In scenarios 1–9, 20-min time windows are considered, in scenarios 10–34, 30 min are considered, and in scenarios 35–59, 40 min. From one scenario to another there is a 5-min variation, reducing the time earlier than desired and consequently increasing the time afterwards. The variation occurs first at pickup, keeping drop-off fixed.

In the 40-min time windows, it was decided to exclude the extremes (35|05 and 05|35), because in the exploratory approach the results were not satisfactory.

4.2   Effects on Desired and Planned Times

One of the decisions to be made is to define an appropriate time window that meets the needs of the different actors in the system. Furthermore, the values found will be decisive for flexibility and must ensure that the temporal distances between the time windows are sufficient to move the vehicle between stops. This part of the study strives to evaluate the effectiveness of simulated scenarios, and to understand the trend with changing parameters and the consequences caused by a given choice.

In Fig. 2 and Fig. 3, a possible representation of the information is presented to analyze the results arising from the modification of the temporal windows in relation to their sizes and their internal divisions. Through these figures, it becomes simpler to compare and examine the discrepancies between each of the scenarios. The graphs have the specified scenarios on the horizontal axis, while the number of orders is on the vertical axis. The bars are subdivided into time intervals, with the size of each bar being related to the number of orders within that interval. The allocation of an order to a slot is determined by the time difference between the planned time and the desired time. By observing the resulting distribution, it is possible to make inferences about the level of user satisfaction. Figure 2 shows the results obtained regarding boarding.

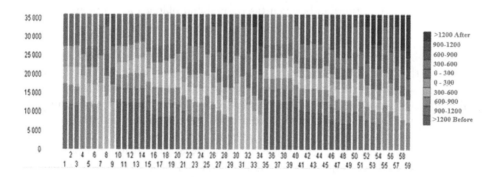

Fig. 2. Relationship between the desired and planned at pickup.

The majority of requests are satisfied before the desired time, as can be seen from the most dominated percentage in the graph. Excluding the first and last time intervals, there is a balance between the intervals. The intermediate ranges are those with the highest percentages. The definition of the time window, especially before what is desired, directly influences the time difference that exists between what is desired and what is predicted, as can be seen in Fig. 2.

Analyzing the effect of the final time windows on boarding, it can be seen that they are not very significant, but it is still noticeable, especially when the difference in time compared to the desired boarding time is smaller. With the reduction in the time difference compared to the desired time, the number of orders that ship earlier decreases, resulting in a transfer of orders to intervals closer to the desired time.

Satisfaction should not be limited to the expected pickup time, but also the expected drop-off time. Figure 3 shows the number of requests that drop-off time in each interval divided by the time difference between the expected and desired arrival time after planning. The most distant intervals continue to have the largest number of requests associated with them, especially those that are later than desired. The number of requests that drop-off time land earlier than desired is lower than those that land later than desired, especially when the later drop-off time to increases in relation to the desired one, presenting here quite significant values in relation to the desired one.

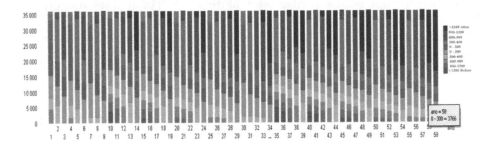

Fig. 3. Relationship between the desired and planned at drop-off

The definition of the time window at drop-off directly influences the time difference that exists between what is desired and what is expected, as can be seen in Fig. 3 with the last time intervals receiving the greatest number of orders. This shows that the insertions of the components corresponding to order landings are pushed back to the limits of the orders that have already been inserted, as a result of which they remain in the last interval and further from what is desired.

Analyzing the effect of the initial time windows on drop off time, it can be seen that they are not very significant, however it is noticeable. With the reduction of the time before the desired pickup of time, the number of requests that are fulfilled closer or in the period after the desired time increases.

Time windows directly influence planning, as depending on the windows used they will influence the placement of orders. The greater the difference between the earliest time you can pickup and the desired time, the greater the difference between the expected and desired time. This fact influences both the initial and final scheduled times, but according to the time window that applies in each part.

The choices of the initial time windows influence the number of orders that are in the most distant interval in time before the desired time at shipment, while the definitions of the final time windows influence the number of orders that are in the most distant time interval after the desired time at unloading. The influence of the initial time windows on landings and the influence of the final time windows on pickup are insignificant compared to the opposite.

The use of different total time windows means that orders are placed further apart in the windows, but there is no difference in the trend of order placement, that is, the larger the time windows are before the desired time, the larger the orders will be placed in the intervals earlier than desired. Therefore, defining the interval before the desired one is more important than defining the total size of the window, as the interval before the desired one influences the expected time of orders more.

Having the scheduled time further away from a desired timeframe can make it easier to accept new orders that are made throughout the day.

5 Conclusion

Decision support systems are increasingly an added value for organisations in an increasingly competitive world. Through DSS tools, relevant and timely information is provided to decision makers to support decision making. The developed tool aims to serve different decision makers, seeking to eliminate part of the work associated with collecting, processing and visualizing data. The visual resources available to decision makers present results calculated according to their specifications and previous perspectives.

These results facilitate understanding in the analysis and enable better decisions. Additionally, decision-makers can ensure that the final solution matches their preferences and the needs of people with reduced mobility by experimenting with various configurations and adjusting parameters as needed. The ultimate goal of the solution is to improve the paratransit system configuration process, empowering decision makers to make more informed and effective decisions.

The data received will allow different decision-makers to identify trends and understand the consequences of their choices, thus making it possible to determine what the best selection should be. Furthermore, it is possible to draw conclusions about the values, taking into account the specificities of the locations and conditions to be implemented. During development, the needs of different decision-makers in terms of information were considered, so that they represent added value and do not prejudice decisions, avoiding the provision of incorrect, incomplete and/or excessive information.

Through the example of which time windows should be applied, we sought to demonstrate how decision-makers can use the tool to support their decisions. However, there are many other variables that can be explored, some with greater weight and complexity. To this end, performance indicators are fundamental and provide support for decisions.

With the current approach, the configuration and decision process essentially rests with the decision makers. However, the next step involves automating some processes aimed at operational and tactical support. This support can be provided by a control and alert system and, in more advanced stages, by identifying specific situations by applying previously established rules to make decisions. Currently, variables present static values in each analysis, but the process must evolve to ranges of values. This would provide decision makers with greater flexibility and lead to a more comprehensive and accurate understanding of the configuration.

Acknowledgments. I declare that the authors have no competing interests.

References

1. Barreto, D.G.: "business Intelligence" Comparação de Ferramentas. Instituto de Informática - Universidade Federal do Rio Grande do Sul (2003)
2. Bouman, R., Dongen, J.V.: Pentaho Solutions Business Intelligence and Data Warehousing with Pentaho and MySQL. Wiley, Indianapolis (2009)
3. Carotenuto, P., Monacelli, D., Raponi, G., Turco, M.: A dynamic simulation model of a flexible transport services for people in congested area. Procedia. Soc. Behav. Sci. **54**, 357–364 (2012). https://doi.org/10.1016/j.sbspro.2012.09.755
4. Carotenuto, P., Paradisi, L., Storchi, G.: A flexible transport service for passengers. Transp. Res. Procedia **3**, 442–451 (2014). https://doi.org/10.1016/j.trpro.2014.10. 025
5. Kimball, R., Caserta, J.: The Data Warehouse ETL Toolkit: Practical Techniques for Extracting, Cleaning, Conforming, and Delivering Data. Wiley, Indianapolis (2004)
6. Lu, W., Quadrifoglio, L., Petrelli, M.: Reliability analysis of centralized versus decentralized zoning strategies for paratransit services. Transp. Res. Procedia **25**, 4100–4113 (2017). https://doi.org/10.1016/j.trpro.2017.05.340
7. Marco, B., Pasquale, C., Giuseppe, R.: Dynamic simulation of a flexible transport system, vol. 14. IFAC (2012). https://doi.org/10.3182/20120523-3-RO-2023.00108
8. Marković, N., Kim, M.E., Schonfeld, P.: Statistical and machine learning approach for planning dial-a-ride systems. Transp. Res. A Policy Pract. **89**, 41–55 (2016). https://doi.org/10.1016/j.tra.2016.05.006
9. Marković, N., Nair, R., Schonfeld, P., Miller-Hooks, E., Mohebbi, M.: Optimizing dial-a-ride services in Maryland: benefits of computerized routing and scheduling. Transp. Res. Part C Emerg. Technol. **55**, 156–165 (2015). https://doi.org/10.1016/ j.trc.2015.01.011
10. McAllister, M.: Success factors of business intelligence. In: 2009 6th IEEE International Working Conference on Mining Software Repositories, p. 283 (2009). https:// doi.org/10.1109/MSR.2009.5069473
11. Mulley, C., Daniels, R.: Quantifying the role of a flexible transport service in reducing the accessibility gap in low density areas: a case-study in north-west sydney. Res. Transp. Bus. Manag. **3**, 12–23 (2012). https://doi.org/10.1016/j.rtbm.2012. 04.006
12. Narayan, J., Cats, O., Oort, N.V., Hoogendoorn, S.: Performance assessment of fixed and flexible public transport in a multi agent simulation framework. Transp. Res. Procedia **27**, 109–116 (2017). https://doi.org/10.1016/j.trpro.2017.12.029
13. Papanikolaou, A., Basbas, S., Mintsis, G., Taxiltaris, C.: A methodological framework for assessing the success of demand responsive transport (DRT) services. Transp. Res. Procedia **24**, 393–400 (2017). https://doi.org/10.1016/j.trpro.2017. 05.095

14. Pensa, S., Masala, E., Arnone, M., Rosa, A.: Planning local public transport: a visual support to decision-making. Procedia. Soc. Behav. Sci. **111**, 596–603 (2014). https://doi.org/10.1016/j.sbspro.2014.01.093
15. Risser, R., Lexell, E.M., Bell, D., Iwarsson, S., Stahl, A.: Use of local public transport among people with cognitive impairments - a literature review. Transport. Res. F Traffic Psychol. Behav. **29**, 83–97 (2015). https://doi.org/10.1016/j.trf.2015.01.002
16. Risser, R., Iwarsson, S., Ståhl, A.: How do people with cognitive functional limitations post-stroke manage the use of buses in local public transport? Transport. Res. F Traffic Psychol. Behav. **15**, 111–118 (2012). https://doi.org/10.1016/j.trf.2011.11.010
17. Syed, S.T., Gerber, B.S., Sharp, L.K.: Traveling towards disease: transportation barriers to health care access. J. Community Health **38**, 976–993 (2013). https://doi.org/10.1007/s10900-013-9681-1
18. Sze, N.N., Christensen, K.M.: Access to urban transportation system for individuals with disabilities. IATSS Res. **41**, 66–73 (2017). https://doi.org/10.1016/j.iatssr.2017.05.002
19. Wong, S.: The limitations of using activity space measurements for representing the mobilities of individuals with visual impairment: a mixed methods case study in the San Francisco bay area. J. Transp. Geogr. **66**, 300–308 (2017). https://doi.org/10.1016/j.jtrangeo.2017.12.004
20. Wright, S., Emele, C.D., Fukumoto, M., Velaga, N.R., Nelson, J.D.: The design, management and operation of flexible transport systems: comparison of experience between UK, Japan and India. Res. Transp. Econ. **48**, 330–338 (2014). https://doi.org/10.1016/j.retrec.2014.09.060
21. Xiang, Z., Chu, C., Chen, H.: A fast heuristic for solving a large-scale static dial-a-ride problem under complex constraints. Eur. J. Oper. Res. **174**, 1117–1139 (2006)

Data Driven Approach to Support the Design of Road Safety Plans in Portuguese Municipalities

Sérgio Pedro Duarte[1]([✉]), João Pedro Maia[2], Miguel Lopes[2], and António Lobo[1]

[1] CITTA -- Centro de Investigação do Território, Transportes e Ambiente, Faculdade de Engenharia da, Universidade do Porto, Porto, Portugal
s.duarte@fe.up.pt

[2] OPT – Optimização e Planeamento de Transportes, S.A, Porto, Portugal

Abstract. Portugal aims to reduce road crashes and fatalities through the implementation of the European Union's Vision Zero strategy. However, for municipalities, choosing effective interventions at a reduced cost is a challenging task. The choice of the proper countermeasures obeys to a series of constraints imposed by local budgets, municipal governments, urban planning strategies, existing infrastructure, and others. To aid decision-makers in designing Municipal Road Safety Plans that maximize safety at reduced costs, a planning approach was built. The proposed approach presents structured sets of countermeasures, linking crash types and site characteristics with potential interventions. The work used real road crash data from three Portuguese municipalities and comprised three stages. First, a cluster analysis to identify and characterize road crashes according to crash type (e.g., vehicle type, number of vehicles) and crash site (e.g., road alignment, cross section, intersection type, visibility). Then, a literature review and an empirical study supported the identification of possible groups of countermeasures for each crash type, and the specification of sets of interventions for each countermeasure group. The final proposal was confirmed by selecting crash hot spots from the original database evaluate if the measures had been correctly assigned to each crash type, providing both exemplification and validation. This work highlights the potential for a structured approach to identify efficient and cost-effective solutions when planning road safety interventions to be included in Municipal Road Safety Plans.

Keywords: road safety · cluster analysis · decision support · policy planning

1 Introduction

Road safety has been a concern for researchers, car manufacturers, road engineers, and policymakers over several decades, and studies have shown the importance of including road safety in long-term planning [1]. Even though great efforts and improvements have been achieved, road crashes and related injuries are still high, with the number of road crashes resulting in injuries or death, recorded in the European Union, being close to

S. P. Duarte et al. (Eds.): ICDSST 2024, LNBIP 506, pp. 70–81, 2024.
https://doi.org/10.1007/978-3-031-59376-5_6

one million, over the last decade [2]. In the urban areas, the growth of urban population as also led to an increase in the road congestion and safety risks associated with a high car-dependency [3, 4], with the number of passenger car still increasing [5]. Recently, the EU has established the Vision Zero roadmap that aims at reaching zero victims by 2050, and developed the Safe System approach, providing a practical framework for achieving that goal [6]. The Safe System is a systemic approach to road safety that considers infrastructure, vehicles, speed, road use, and post-crash care.

In the Portuguese context, the Vision Zero strategy increased municipalities' awareness regarding road safety and Municipal Road Safety Plans (Planos Municipais de Segurança Rodoviária - PMSR) are being updated. These plans include a strategic intervention plan for the following five years; therefore, municipalities face the challenge of budget allocation. On the one hand, complex countermeasures can be efficient, but expensive, and excessively designed considering the crash risks. On the other hand, simple and low-cost solutions may not solve the targeted problem as desired. For those reasons, decisionmakers must select cost-effective countermeasures that target the specific problems registered in their municipality. Due to budget limitations, other than selecting effective countermeasures, municipalities want to select intervention sites that are more likely to offer a safety increase.

Although current literature presents studies on countermeasures and risk factors [7, 8], this extensive list does not consider the trends of a specific site. For instance, important contributions have resulted from projects such as SafetyCube project [9]. The project, funded within the Horizons 2020 Programme of the European Commission, gathered experienced road safety experts from different European countries and produced a DSS to support evidence-based policy making. The SafetyCube DSS is the European Road Safety Decision Support System that provides important insights regarding the positive impacts of the different countermeasures, for the different transport modes and road users, but the DSS does not consider different crash types.

By proposing a data driven approach, our goal is to help policymakers in creating a prioritized intervention plan that not only links countermeasures to road infrastructure, but also to crash characteristics. For instance, a site that has registered mostly single-vehicle crashes will require different interventions than if that same site had registered multiple-vehicle crashes. While both can gain from better lane markings, the first can be a result of poor shoulder conditions, and the second a result of poor visibility due to road alignment.

Considering the above, we have developed an approach that can be adapted into a decision support methodology or evolve into a decision support tool. The proposed approach resorts to available road crash data to create categories and characterize road crash types. Then, countermeasures are associated with the types of crashes.

As this is an exploratory work with a small database, one cannot affirm that a decision support tool was developed, rather an approach that supports intervention planning. To evolve into a complete DSS, more crash types would have to be identified in other municipalities. Thus, this paper focuses on exploring the conceptual approach and provides examples of its application to hotspots in the three municipalities. First, Sect. 2 describes the methods and data used throughout this study; after, Sect. 3 presents the results, including the crash types and groups of countermeasures; and Sect. 4 depicts a potential application of the approach with the selection of specific countermeasures. Finally, some learned lessons and limitation are discussed in Sect. 5.

2   Methods and Data

The work presented in this paper had two input sources from which we obtained three outputs, that together form a sequence of actions (see Fig. 1) that support the interventions to include in the PMSR. Figure 1 is a schematic representation of the research tasks (vertical sequences) that led to the proposed decision-making approach (horizontal sequence). The scheme includes sources (light grey) and outputs (dark grey), as well as intermediate tasks performed in this research (outlined boxes). In this section, we start by presenting the three municipalities used for the study and proceed with a description of the methods and data used in each step.

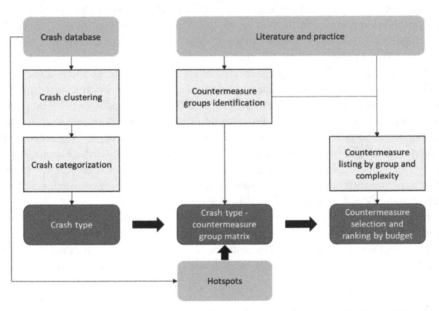

Fig. 1. Research methodology (vertically) and proposed approach (horizontally).

2.1   Data Description

This study was supported by real data from three municipalities: Castelo Branco, Loures, and Vila Real, that represent different contexts regarding geographical location and land-use. The three municipalities provide an interesting mix, not only between Portuguese regions, but also in urban profile, ranging between a consolidated urban core surrounded by very low-density territories, as in Castelo Branco (52 291 inhabitants; 36 inh/km^2), a fragmented urbanized pattern, as in Vila Real (49 574 inhabitants; 131 inh/km^2), and a dense suburban setting with a metropolitan area, as is the case of Loures (201 590 inhabitants; 1 205 inh/km^2). The different urban profiles are connected by different road networks, and the different economic activities generate different travel patterns, leading to different crash registers, as visible in Table 1. The data represents road crashes between 2016 and 2021 for Castelo Branco, and between 2017 and 2021 for Loures and Vila Real.

Table 1. Number of observations for each municipality, by type of victim.

Municipality	Number of observations				
	Slightly Injured	Severely Injured	Fatalities	Total	Per 1000 in-habitants
Castelo Branco	606	129	20	727	13,9
Vila Real	774	54	15	825	16,7
Loures	3 157	142	40	3 293	16,4

The municipal plans PMSR only consider roads managed by municipalities, but the database registered all road crashes. Therefore, road crashes that had occurred in other road types (e.g., motorways) were removed from the database. The variables were collected from standardized police reports that are mandatory to fill in case of crashes with injuries and/or fatalities. Despite the standard form, the form was not uniformly filled-in, thus the available variables would vary. In total, there were 54 variables filled-in at least of the database, either present and the police report, or added by the municipalities.

Considering the information that we could extract from the variables, data was treated and a final list of variables was obtained. Further, we gathered the variables in four dimensions, to easily characterize road crashes. Table 2 presents the list of variables and the databases where they are available. It is noticeable that Loures has the least information regarding geometry and site characteristics (12 variables in total), while Vila Real has poor information regarding the type of vehicle involved in the crash (17 variables in total), and Castelo Branco is the most complete database (19 variables in total).

2.2 Crash Clustering and Categorization

The main objective of this task was to identify the types of crashes that had been registered in each of the municipalities, and to evaluate if there were any similarities between the municipalities. To do so, we performed a Partitioning Around Medoids (PAM) clustering analysis with Gower distance, using the three databases provided by the municipalities. This method was selected for the characteristics of the data and for its performance in similar studies [10, 11]. For this, we used the cluster package of the software R [12].

As there were significant differences regarding the available variables (Table 2), we conducted three separated cluster analyses, one for each municipality. The number of clusters was determined using the silhouette coefficient (SC), that considers the average distance between observations in the same cluster and the distance to the nearest cluster.

Table 2. Variables by Municipality

	Variable	Castelo Branco	Vila Real	Loures
Crash	Injury type	x	x	x
	Light vehicle	x		x
	Two-wheel vehicle	x		x
	Heavy/other vehicle	x		x
	Crash nature	x	x	x
Context and (surrounding) environment	Weekend	x	x	x
	Luminosity	x	x	x
	Environment	x	x	x
	Adherence	x	x	x
	Road hierarchy	x	x	x
Geometry	Horizontal alignment	x	x	
	Vertical alignment	x	x	
	Shoulder	x	x	
	Intersection	x	x	x
Crash site	Direction	x	x	
	Lane markings	x	x	x
	Vertical signs	x	x	
	Pavement	x	x	
	Traffic lights	x	x	
	Lanes		x	

For a certain number of clusters, the highest the value of SC, the better the cluster performance. Therefore, the selection of the number of clusters should consider, the maximum value of SC and, at the same time, the interpretability of the results, since the smaller the number of clusters the less information is obtained from the analysis, which, in some cases, points to a local maximum of the SC.

To ensure generalization of road crashes, we performed one test with a unified database with the 20 variables, with observations from the three municipalities, since PAM clustering allows for missing values. As the road crash types were similar as the ones found when studying the municipalities in separate, we opted to keep them separate to not loose detail in the characterization.

2.3   Countermeasure Groups and Matrix

The second major task of this work was the identification of countermeasures that could be later associated with crash types. This was performed in two steps: a list of measures was created based on a literature review, with a total of 50 measures; the listed measures were organized in groups, according to the type of intervention (signaling, reprofiling, policy/education, etc.

The assignment of each measure in a group allows for a better support of policymakers, who can, in a first approach, select the type of measure according to the available budget, before making a detailed decision. The groups of measures were adapted from an existing intervention hierarchy used by OPT – Optimização e Planeamento de Transportes, S.A., that considers five types of interventions during the design of PMSR, and complemented with other types of measures found in the literature. OPT's groups include: complete reprofiling, traffic calming, traffic lights, public illumination, horizontal and vertical signs.

After the literature review, the groups of measures considered in this work were:

- RBE – regulation, behavior, and education (e.g., red light cameras, education - hazard perception training, awareness raising and campaigns, road safety audits and inspections);
- SMR – signage and marking reinforcement (e.g., implementation of rumble strips at centerline, traffic sign installation and/or maintenance, variable message signs, road markings implementation at junctions);
- SpC – speed control measures (e.g., school zones, reduction of speed limit, installation of speed humps);
- PI – public illumination (e.g., installation of lighting & improvements to existing lighting);
- TL – traffic lights (e.g., signalized crosswalks, traffic signal installation, traffic signal reconfiguration)
- PR – partial reprofiling (e.g., implementation of narrowings, implementation of traffic calming schemes, increase lane width, change shoulder type, implementation of sidewalks);
- CR – complete reprofiling (creation of bypass roads, road surface treatments, increase number of lanes, change junction type).

Finally, these groups were assigned to the road crash types identified before as possible interventions. First, for every crash type the vulnerable road user (VRU) was identified (pedestrian or motorcyclist), when possible. Since car drivers are not considered vulnerable, it is important to note that in single-vehicle collisions, involving light vehicles (cars), there is no vulnerable road user identified. Then, a possible cause of the crash was determined based on the variable categories of each crash type. For instance, if a cluster groups vehicle-pedestrian collisions, which occur mostly during the day, there is no need to install or improve public illumination, but rather, improve crossing conditions.

The assignment of a group to each crash type, allows for filtering the measures from the total list, and policymakers can then select the measures that better fit specific sites, as it will be demonstrated in the last section of this paper.

3   Crash Types

The clustering process resulted in four clusters for Castelo Branco (SC = 0.170), five for Vila Real (SC = 0.133), and five for Loures (SC = 0.345). This process provided 14 crash types that were characterized according to the dimensions previously established. After a first observation, it is visible that all the municipalities presented, at least one cluster formed with each crash nature, resulting in a total of six multiple-vehicle collision crash types, six single-vehicle collision crash types, and two pedestrian-vehicle collision crash types.

The crash types are presented by crash nature, namely: single-vehicle collisions (Table 3), multiple vehicle collisions (Table 4), and vehicle-pedestrian collisions (Table 5). For each dimension, the tables present the dominant value for the variables related to that dimension, except for the "crash" dimension, because "crash nature" together with the type of vehicle involved are the main characteristics of the crash type. Regarding the type of injury, there was not cluster representing severe injuries nor fatalities, thus light injuries were dominant in all clusters.

Table 3. Single vehicle collisions.

Crash type	SV1	SV2	SV3	SV4	SV5	SV6
Vehicle type	Light	N/A	N/A	Light	Two-wheel	Two-wheel
Context and environment	Weekend	Weekend	Weekend	Weekend	Weekend	Weekend
	Day	Day	Day	Night	Day	Day
	Rural	Rural	Urban	Urban	Urban	Urban
	Dry	Wet	Dry	Dry	Dry	Dry
	Main road	Main road	Main road	Main road	Local road	Local road
Crash site	N/A	2 + lanes	1 lane	N/A	N/A	N/A
	Asphalt	Asphalt	Asphalt	N/A	Asphalt	N/A
	2-way road	1 way road	2-way road	N/A	2-way road	N/A
	LM	LM	No LM	N/A	LM	N/A
	No VS	No VS	No VS	N/A	No VS	N/A
	No TL	No TL	No TL	N/A	No TL	N/A
Road geometry	Straight	Curve	Curve	N/A	Curve	N/A
	Flat	Slope	Slope	N/A	Flat	N/A
	NS	Paved sh	NS	N/A	Paved sh	N/A
	Segment	Segment	Segment	Segment	Segment	Segment

N/A not available; LM – lane markings; VS – vertical sign; TL – traffic light; NS – no shoulder; sh. – shoulder.

The dominant category was selected by observing the percentage of observations with that value. There were only three situations where there were two categories with similar percentage. In those cases, we registered both (crash type MV1, MV5, PV2).

Even before assigning vulnerable road users and possible crash causes, the information extracted from these tables can be already used for the city diagnosis. Note, for instance, the case of PV1, referring to vehicle- pedestrian collisions (run over) on sites where there are crosswalk signs and lane markings. Other important takeaways from this step are: all single vehicle collisions happen during the weekend and crashes involving two wheeled vehicles occur on local road.

Although the crash types resulting from Loures' clusters provide less information regarding geometry, there is still valuable insights on those crash types, such as the case of MV5 and MV6 that refer to multiple vehicle collisions that occur in both local and main road, with wet pavement.

Table 4. Multiple vehicle collisions.

Crash type	MV1	MV2	MV3	MV4	MV5	MV6
Vehicle type	Light	N/A	N/A	N/A	Light	Light
Context and environment	Weekday	Weekday	Weekday	Weekday	Weekday	Weekday
	Day	Day	Day	Day	Day	Day
	Urban	Urban	Urban	Urban	Urban	Urban
	Dry	Dry	Dry	Dry	Wet	Wet
	Local road	Local road	Main road	Main road	Local road	Main road
Crash site	N/A	1 lane	2 + lanes	1 lane	N/A	N/A
	Asphalt	Asphalt	Asphalt	Asphalt	N/A	N/A
	2-way	2-way	1-way	2-way	N/A	N/A
	LM	LM	LM	LM	N/A	N/A
	Stop and Yield / Other VS	No VS	No VS	No VS	N/A	N/A
	No TL	No TL	No TL	No TL	N/A	N/A
Road geometry	Straight	Straight	Straight	Straight	N/A	N/A
	Slope	Flat	Flat	Flat	N/A	N/A
	Paved sh	Paved sh. / NS	Paved sh	Paved sh	N/A	N/A
	Intersec	Segment	Segment	Segment	Segment /intersec	Segment

N/A not available; LM – lane markings; VS – vertical sign; TL – traffic light; NS – no shoulder; sh. – shoulder.

4 Countermeasure Selection

The crash types characterized allowed to identify the vulnerable road user (VRU), and potential causes for the crashes. Although this was an empirical process, thus requiring validation with further information, it provides interesting perspective for the decision-makers. The VRU is the driver in the case of single-vehicle collisions with two-wheeled vehicles, and the pedestrian in vehicle-pedestrian collisions.

Let us consider, for instance, the case of SV4 crash types: that involve light vehicles and happen during the weekends, at night, on urban and dry main roads. Assuming that during weekends there is less traffic volume, one can infer that: (1) being driving on a main road, the driver is over speeding or, (2) there are poor light conditions as it is nighttime. Consequently, there are two feasible solutions for preventing the crash: either speed control measures are implemented, or public illumination is improved. After this analysis, the crash types and the groups of measures were matched in a crash-measure group matrix (Table 6).

Table 5. Vehicle-pedestrian collisions.

Crash type	PV1	PV2
Vehicle type	Light	Light
Context and environment	Weekday	Weekday
	Day	Day
	Urban	Urban
	Dry	Dry
	Local road	Local road
Crash site	N/A	N/A
	Asphalt	N/A
	2-way	N/A
	LM	N/A
	Crosswalk	N/A
	No TL	N/A
Road geometry	Straight	N/A
	Flat	N/A
	Paved sh	N/A
	Segment	Segment/intersection

N/A not available; LM – lane markings; VS – vertical sign; TL – traffic light; NS – no shoulder; sh. – shoulder.

Other causes for crashing were found to be visibility in the case of multiple vehicle collisions on slopes or curves, poor road profile design when there is no shoulder for single vehicle collisions, or in intersections for multiple vehicle collisions. For vehicle

Table 6. Crash-measure group matrix.

Crash type	RBE	SMR	SpC	PI	TL	PR	CR
SV1			x			x	x
SV2		x		x		x	x
SV3	x	x	x	x		x	x
SV4		x		x			
SV5	x	x				x	
SV6	x	x				x	
MV1				x	x	x	x
MV2		x	x			x	x
MV3		x	x			x	x
MV4		x	x			x	x
MV5	x	x	x				
MV6	x	x	x				
PV1	x		x	x	x	x	
PV2	x	x	x	x	x	x	

pedestrian-collisions, besides the possibility of improving horizontal and vertical signs for increased awareness of crossing sites, it is of utmost importance to implement speed and traffic control solutions, such as traffic lights.

The measures from the group Regulation, Behavior and Education are always important, but even more when increased awareness is necessary towards VRU. Therefore, these measures are most suitable for SV5, SV6, PV1, and PV2. Nevertheless, they can also be used in cases where speeding is a possible cause for crashes.

After finding the appropriate group of measures, the decision-maker has access to a detailed list of measures, from the 50 previously identified, and may select the ones that better fit the specific site and the available budget. For instance, for partial reprofiling, safety barriers will be more suitable for single-vehicle collisions, and refuge islands for vehicle-pedestrian collisions. For that specific group of measures, the list mentions the following measures:

- Safety barriers installation;
- Change type of safety barriers;
- Increase lane width;
- Change median type;
- Sight distance treatments;
- Implementation of traffic calming schemes;
- Change shoulder type;
- Improve skewness or junction angle;
- Implementation of narrowing's;
- Implementation of 30-Zones;

- Implementation of refuge islands;
- Implementation of sidewalks.

To ensure that our matrix was linked to real cases, we compared a real case from an identified hotspot in the three municipalities. For the purpose of this paper, we will use the case of Vila Real as an example. The hotspot had registered five crashes in the junction between Santa Iria Street and Largo Santa Iria. The observations of the registered crashes were analyzed, and it was confirmed that all crashes would fall into MV1 crash type as the observations pointed to the presence of vertical signs, near intersections, in a slope. As so, using Google street view, we compared how the site was in the last years, and we were able to verify that the junction was transformed into a roundabout, that is one of the measures of the group Complete reprofiling, specifically "Convert junction to roundabout", thus confirming that our approach would reach a similar result.

5 Conclusions

While it is important to co-design mobility and transport policies under the Sustainable Urban Mobility Plans guidelines, with the participation of different players, some interventions can be better planned if a proper diagnosis of the safety within the urban space is available. Citizens should share their perception on sidewalk safety, as it increases their comfort, but when it comes to allocate budget, it is important to make prudent decisions to plan interventions where it is most needed. That diagnosis can come from a data driven approach such as the one described in this paper.

The proposed approach considers, on one hand, the types of crashes and, on the other hand, possible interventions for improving road safety. Interventions can be prioritized according to preidentified hotspots, available budget, and priorities. Although the hotspots used in this paper were considered only as a validation, they were being used by the municipalities to establish priorities, using the number of crashes as an indicator for hazard zones. In total, 14 road crashes were identified: six single-vehicle collision, six multiple-vehicle collisions, and two pedestrian-vehicle collisions. For each crash type, we identified possible interventions, assuming possible crash cause.

The empirical association of crash cause to crash type is a limitation of our work since the real cause was not registered in the database. However, we compared the intervention type suggested by our approach to interventions that took place in a recent past and could confirm that the intervention was of the same type of the one our approach would suggest. Hence, future works could be expanding this approach to other municipalities as a way to better test the existing crash types, and possibly finding new ones. In sum, this work can be a first step to develop a policy design approach, or it can be expanded with new crash types until the crash type-measure group itself becomes a support tool for policymakers.

Acknowledgments. This research was funded in part by the Fundação para a Ciência e a Tecnologia, I.P. (FCT, Funder ID = 50110000187) under the grant with DOI 10.54499/CEECINST/00010/2021/CP1770/CT0003. The authors thank OPT for the collaboration in this study and facilitating access to crash databases.

Disclosure of Interests.. The authors have no competing interests to declare that are relevant to the content of this article.

References

1. Ferreira, S., Couto, A.: Categorical modeling to evaluate road safety at the planning level. J. Transp. Saf. Secur. **4**(4), 308–322 (2012)
2. ERSO, European Road Safety Observatory (2020) Roads," no. 2020, pp. 1–41, 2020
3. Silva, P.B., Andrade, M., Ferreira, S.: Machine learning applied to road safety modeling: A systematic literature review, J. Traffic Transp. Eng. English Ed., **7**(6), 775–790 (2020)
4. Coppola, P., Lobo, A.: Inclusive and collaborative advanced transport: are we really heading to sustainable mobility? Eur. Transp. Res. Rev. **14**(1), 1–6 (2022)
5. European Union, Statistical Pocketbook 2021 - EU Transport in figures (2021)
6. European Commission, EU Road Safety Policy Framework 2021–2030 - Next steps towards, Vision Zero (2019)
7. Papadimitriou, E., Filtness, A., Theofilatos, A., Ziakopoulos, A., Quigley, C., Yannis, G.: Review and ranking of crash risk factors related to the road infrastructure. Accid. Anal. Prev. **125**(February), 85–97 (2019)
8. Papadimitriou, E., Theofilatos, A.: Meta-analysis of crash-risk factors in freeway entrance and exit areas. J. Transp. Eng. Part A Syst. **143**(10), 1–10 (2017)
9. Martensen, H., et al., The European road safety decision support system on risks and measures, Accid. Anal. Prev., **125**, 344–351 (2019)
10. Soares, S., Lobo, A., Ferreira, S., Cunha, L., Couto, A.: Takeover performance evaluation using driving simulation: a systematic review and meta-analysis. Eur. Transp. Res. Rev. **13**(1), 1–18 (2021). https://doi.org/10.1186/s12544-021-00505-2
11. Duarte, S.P., Lobo, A., Ribeiro, J., Neves, J.V., Couto, A., Ferreira, S.: A multilevel decision-making approach for road infrastructure management. J. Decis. Syst. **00**(00), 1–23 (2023)
12. R Core Team, R: A language and environment for statistical computing. R foundation for statistical computing. https://www.r-project.org/. (Accessed: 28-May-2022)

Decision Factors

Performance of Holistic Evaluation for Multi-criteria Decisions Comparing Selection or Elimination of Alternatives

Tarsila Rani Soares de Vasconcelos[ID], Lucia Reis Peixoto Roselli[✉][ID], and Adiel Teixeira de Almeida[ID]

Center for Decision Systems and Information Development (CDSID), Universidade Federal de Pernambuco, Recife, PE, Brazil

tarsila.vasconcelos@ufpe.br, {lrpr,almeida}@cdsid.org.br

Abstract. In some decision situations, the use of Multi-Criteria Decision-Making/Aiding methods cannot capture the real cognitive process performed by Decision-Makers. In this context, behavioral studies can be performed to investigate Decision-Makers' behavior during the decision process. This study has been undertaken to compare previous studies in order to investigate how Decision-Makers performed holistic evaluations using graphical and tabular visualization presented in the FITradeoff Decision Support System. Results may be applied to other methods using additive aggregation in the MAVT (Multi-Attribute Value Theory) context. The study aims to modify or transform the method based on the inclusion of behavioral aspects observed during the decision process. Thus, in this study an experiment has been designed to conduct holistic evaluations. Eight visualizations are presented arranged in bar graphs and tables, and two decision processes have been investigated – the selection of the best alternative and the elimination of the worst alternative. The experiment has been applied to 134 participants, and the data were collected and analyzed in terms of their probabilities of success and preferences.

Keywords: Multi-Criteria Decision Making/Aiding (MCDM/A) · Holistic evaluation · Behavioral experiment · FITradeoff Method

1 Introduction

Multi-Attribute Value Theory (MAVT) [1] is one of the best-known theories of the Multi-Criteria Decision-Making/Aiding (MCDM/A) approach. In methods which follow MAVT concepts, additive aggregation of consequences is performed in order to obtain the global value of each one of the alternatives [2, 3]. In this type of aggregation, the Decision-Makers (DMs) have a compensatory rationality concerning making tradeoffs between the consequences [4].

In MCDM/A there are two preference modeling paradigms: elicitation by decomposition, in which DMs perform the preference modelling in the consequences space; and

S. P. Duarte et al. (Eds.): ICDSST 2024, LNBIP 506, pp. 85–97, 2024.
https://doi.org/10.1007/978-3-031-59376-5_7

holistic evaluation, in which DMs perform the preference modelling in the alternatives space [5, 6].

In the literature, there are three types of uses of holistic evaluations. They can be used for preference disaggregation, to add more information or to finalize the decision process [3, 6, 7]. Holistic judgments used for the purpose of preference disaggregation are mostly applied in UTA (UTilitè Additive) methods, where they enable an indirect estimation of the parameters of the model [7, 8].

As for the last two types, the FITradeoff (Flexible and Interactive Tradeoff) method is one method that combines both uses [5, 6]. Some applications with the FITradeoff method present the use of holistic evaluation to add information or to finalize the decision process [9–17].

In the context of holistic evaluations, the DM has the possibility of comparing options directly by using the alternatives space, i.e., they can state, explicitly, that one alternative is preferable to another [6]. Although not all authors use the terminology "holistic evaluation", it is nevertheless considered in many studies because the alternatives are presented as a whole, by virtue of their being used to make a global evaluation, and they are not analyzed in each criterion separately [18].

To enable alternatives to be compared in holistic evaluations, in the FITradeoff method, graphical and tabular visualizations can be used, since they support the DMs to better understand the performance of alternatives in a specific MCDM/A problem [6]. According to de Almeida [18], holistic judgments based on graphic visualizations are a way of reducing the decision problem and saving the DM time and effort.

In this context, with the purpose of analyzing how DMs perform the holistic evaluation of alternatives, an experiment with graphical and tabular visualizations was developed and applied. This experiment has been applied to investigate DMs' behavior when they express preferences in the space of alternatives. This study builds on the previous one [20] that aims to modify or transform the FITradeoff method based on the inclusion of behavioral aspects observed during the decision process [19].

Therefore, this study aims to improve decision-making processes with regard to using holistic evaluation to finalize or add information in MCDM/A methods in the context of MAVT.

The paper is structured as follows. Section 2 discusses some previous studies in the literature on holistic evaluation. Section 3 describes the experiment and the system that was developed. Section 4 presents the results; Sect. 5 discusses the findings of this analysis and Sect. 6 presents the conclusions and makes suggestions for future lines of research.

2 Previous Studies on This Line of Research

Before introducing the specific purpose of this paper, an overview of previous studies on this line of research is presented as follows.

Considering MCDM/A methods, they cannot capture the real cognitive process performed by DMs and may generate solutions that do not correctly represent their preferences [21]. These studies aim to improve the FITradeoff Decision Support System

(DSS) and to improve the FITradeoff method and offer insights for improvements in decision-making processes in general.

In this context, behavioral and neuroscience studies have been conducted since 2017 in order to investigate DMs' behavior when the FITradeoff method is applied. Several experiments have been constructed to investigate the two paradigms of preference modeling –holistic evaluation [22–31] and elicitation by decomposition [32–35].

Experiments involving holistic evaluations present different types of visualizations to investigate how DMs use them to perform a holistic evaluation. The first experiments compare three types of graphs: bar graph, spider graph and bubble graph [29–31]. After that, the next experiments included the comparison of tables versus bar graphs [26–28]. The first experiments used only Eye-Tracking; the other experiments included the Electroencephalogram (EEG) complement the studies. Due to the Covid-19 pandemic, online surveys have been developed to continue the studies considering only behavioral issues. In this context, a system was developed in order to enable the experiments to be conducted and it was called BASHE - Behavioral Analysis System by Holistic Evaluation. The experiments conducted using the BASHE are the focus of this paper, presented in the next section. All experiments involving the holistic evaluation paradigm aim to investigate how DMs evaluate MCDM/A problems when these are represented by tabular and graphical visualizations in order to express a dominance relation between the alternatives.

Concerning to the experiments performed to investigate the elicitation by decomposition [32–35], they have been conducted to evaluates the cognitive effort demanded during the elicitation process performed in FITradeoff method [5, 6]. More details can be found in the papers already published in literature. This paper discusses an experiment performed to investigate the holistic evaluation paradigm.

Based on previous studies, improvements have been made in the FITradeoff DSS. For instance, the holistic evaluation phase is incorporated not only into the choice problematic, but also into the ranking [36] and sorting problematics [37]. As to the interaction with the analyst to improve the FITradeoff decision process, the findings from previous studies led to the creation of the Success-Based Decision Rule, which aims to support analysts in the process of advising the DM on whether or not to carry out their analysis holistically [22].Modulations have been done in other methods and decision support systems based behavioral and neuroscience studies [38–43], being a megatrend in MCDM/A field [44].

Therefore, the purpose of this particular study is to continue examining holistic evaluation in order to provide insights for the analyst on how best to advise DMs and to generate more improvements in the design aspect for the FITradeoff DSS, in general. Hence, the following sections will present the specific results arising from the experiment conducted.

3   Experiment

The system named BASHE (Behavioral Analysis System by Holistic Evaluation) was developed to conduct the kind of experiment discussed in this paper. Its functions include presenting the holistic visualizations and collecting data from the participants.

The experiment performed using the BASHE consisted of presenting 2 decision problems, which did not have an explicit application context, divided into 8 visualizations. These problems showed alternatives evaluated on criteria, where the performance of each alternative on these criteria varied between 0 and 1. The data were presented in 4 tables and 4 bar graphs, and the participants had to evaluate and select the best alternative or eliminate the worst one, depending on the case.

All problems had three alternatives which were evaluated against five criteria. The weights of the criteria were distributed in two forms, same weights, and different weights, the latter being defined according to an arithmetic progression. Criterion 1 had the highest weight value and Criterion 5 had the lowest weight value. Therefore, the participants (DMs) had to analyze the alternatives and to select the best alternative or eliminate the worst one in each case.

The correct answers for each question were previously computed using MAVT theory. In other words, the DMs had to consider a compensatory rationality to select the alternative with the highest overall value or eliminate the alternative with the lowest overall value. In addition, a difference in overall value (global value) from one alternative to another have been recognized as 5%. At the begging, a difference in 10% and 15% have been tested, but it becomes very easy to select the best alternative.

The overall value of alternative a, V(a), can be calculated according to Eq. (1) where w_i is the weight of criterion i and $v_i(a)$ is the marginal value function [1].

$$V(a) = \sum_{i=1}^{n} w_i v_i(a) \tag{1}$$

Two examples of questions considered in the survey are presented in Fig. 1. It is important emphasize that acronyms have been used to represent the visualizations. Considering the two examples of Fig. 1, Sel 3A5C TS represents that DMs should select (Sel) the best alternative of a table (T) with three alternatives (3A) evaluated in five criteria (5C), the weights of which have the same values (S), while Eli 3A5C BD represents that DMs should eliminate (Elim) the worst alternative of a bar graph (B) and the weights have different values (D).

It is worth noting that the eight visualizations are showed in a random order. A random order has been used to present the visualizations for participants since in a previous study was observed that a random sequence of visualizations leads to better results [27]. The order than the visualizations have been showed is described in Table 1.

For the entire experiment, a time restriction of 15 min was used, and participants were informed of this before the questions were shown, but no timer was displayed on screen. It should be mentioned that it was not possible to return to review the questions or modify the option after the alternative had been chosen. All participants received the same instructions to perform the experiment.

In addition, a behavioral questionnaire was also applied in order to collect the participants' preferences and perceptions about the experiment. After the experiment, without there being a limit of 15 min, participants were required to answer a set of 11 Behavioral Questions (BQ) and the results from this included being able to collect their preferences for each type of question and their level of exhaustion when performing the experiment.

Example 1 – Sel 3A5C TS   Example 2 – Eli 3A5C BD

Weights	0.2	0.2	0.2	0.2	0.2
Alt/Crit	Crit1	Crit2	Crit3	Crit4	Crit5
Alt1	0.6	0.55	0.79	1	1
Alt2	1	0.38	1	0.76	0.82
Alt3	0.78	1	0.49	0.56	0.62

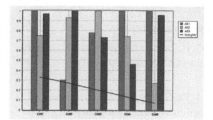

Fig. 1. Examples of visualizations used in the experiment

Initially, the participants were students at the Federal University of Pernambuco (UFPE) and then the experiment was extended to other universities. The survey was applied to 134 students, of whom 45% identify with the female gender, 43% with the male gender and 12% identify with another gender or preferred not to answer the question on gender identity. It should be mentioned that all participants performed the experiment with similar conditions and received the same instructions before starting.

4   Results

One of the metrics analyzed was the average percentage of participants who correctly selected the best alternative or eliminated the worst one. This is called the Hit Rate (HR). Therefore, given HR values between 0% and 100%, the probabilities of success (π) between 0 and 1 are obtained, as well as the standard deviations (σ) which are computed following the Bernoulli distribution [22]. Table 1 presents these results.

Table 1. Results of each visualization

Visualization	π	σ
Eli 3A5C BS	0.62	0.49
Sel 3A5C TD	0.41	0.49
Sel 3A5C TS	0.46	0.50
Eli 3A5C BD	0.34	0.47
Eli 3A5C TS	0.61	0.49
Eli 3A5C TD	0.32	0.47
Sel 3A5C BD	0.44	0.50
Sel 3A5C BS	0.37	0.48

Combining the probability of success of each one of the visualizations and the answers for two questions of the behavioral questionnaire (Q2 and Q4), illustrated in Table 2, four statistical tests have been performed to investigate if the participants who prefers one kind of visualization really presented a better performance in them.

Table 2. Q2 and Q4 of the behavioral questionnaire

Behavioral Questions	Options of answers
Q2. Regarding the forms of visualization, which configuration did you prefer?	• Tabular • Bar graph • No answer
Q4. Regarding the type of problem, which configuration did you prefer?	• Selecting the best alternative • Eliminating the worst alternative • No answer

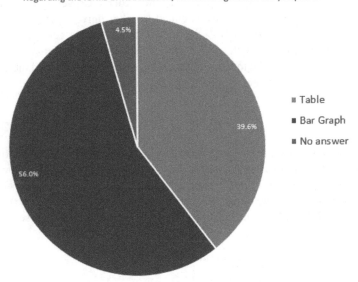

Regarding the forms of visualization, which configuration did you prefer?

4.5%
39.6%
56.0%

■ Table
■ Bar Graph
■ No answer

Fig. 2. Preference for tables or bar graphs

Test 1:

- H0: Participants who preferred to analyze tables had similar probabilities of success than participants who preferred to analyze bar graphs.
- H1: Participants who preferred to analyze tables had different probabilities of success by analyzing tables than by analyzing bar graphs.

Test 2:

- H0: Participants who preferred to analyze bar graphs had similar probabilities of success than participants who preferred to analyze tables.
- H1: Participants who preferred to analyze bar graphs had different probabilities of success by analyzing bar graphs than by analyzing tables.

Test 3:

- H0: Participants who preferred to select the best alternative had similar probabilities of success by selecting than by eliminating.
- H1: Participants who preferred to select the best alternative had different probabilities of success by selecting than by eliminating.

Test 4:

- H0: Participants who preferred to eliminate the worst alternative had similar probabilities of success by eliminating than by selecting alternatives.
- H1: Participants who preferred to eliminate the worst alternative had different probabilities of success by eliminating than by selecting alternatives.

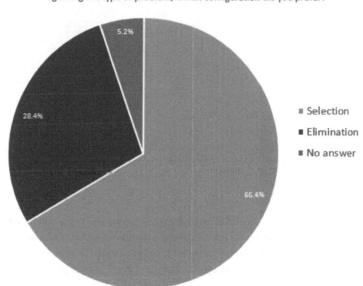

Regarding the type of problem, which configuration did you prefer?

5.2%

28.4%

66.4%

- Selection
- Elimination
- No answer

Fig. 3. Preference for selection or elimination

To conduct the tests, firstly, groups of participants were determined. These groupings and their probabilities of success are shown in Table 3 and Table 4.

Table 3. Probability of success considering preferences for tables or bar graphs

Participants' preferences	π of table	π of bar graph
Who preferred Table	0.43	0.46
Who preferred Bar graph s	0.47	0.44

Table 4. Probability of success considering preferences for selection or elimination

Participants' preferences	π of selection	π of elimination
Who preferred to Select	0.45	0.46
Who preferred to Eliminate	0.39	0.53

For the tests of the hypotheses, it was observed that the set of answers was not normally distributed. So, the Wilcoxon signed rank test for paired samples (V) was used. For a significance level of 0.05, none of the four null hypotheses were rejected.

Table 5. Results of hypothesis tests

Hypothesis	P-value
Test 1	0.584
Test 2	0.3162
Test 3	0.5851
Test 4	0.05471

5   Discussion

Based on Table 1, it can be seen that selection questions have a higher probability of success than elimination questions for different weights and that elimination questions have a higher probability of success than selection questions for equal weights. Furthermore, comparing the performance of tables and bar graphs, their probability of success is similar, in general.

Thus, by analyzing only the probabilities of success, it can be seen that the results of this study are consistent with those presented in [23], which investigates the same visualizations but using another system with a different population.

Based on Tables 4 and 5, an interesting result is suggested. It can be seen that the participants had a slightly higher probability of success in visualizations which are not preferred in the behavioral questions. For instance, most of the participants prefer to use bar graphs (Fig. 2), but they presented a higher probability of success using tables. In addition, the participants who preferred tables had a higher probability of success using bar graphs, as illustrated in Table 3. The same phenomenon is observed in Table 4, most of the participants preferred to select the best alternative than to eliminate the worst one (Fig. 3), but they performed better when eliminating the worst alternative.

This is an interesting result, even based only in descriptive analysis. It can suggest that maybe DMs can prefer an aspect which may not be the best for them or that DMs answered the preferential survey in a different way that nevertheless was used to conduct the holistic evaluation experiment. This phenomenon should be a point of attention for the analyst during the advising process with DMs.

The only exception is the group of participants who preferred to eliminate the worst alternative. They really did have a higher probability of success by eliminating alternatives than by selecting them. This is emphasized by the p-value of H4, which is the highest in comparison with the p-values of the other hypotheses (Table 5).

Otherwise, the statistical inference showed that none of the four null hypotheses were rejected, as illustrated in Table 5. For instance, for test 3, it can be said with 95% confidence that DMs who prefer to select the best alternative presented similar performance when evaluating selection problems and elimination problems. In this context, the effect suggested in the descriptive analysis is not observed in the statistical tests. Therefore, more studies should be done to compare these groups to investigate the phenomenon observed in descriptive analysis.

6 Conclusion

This study presented an experiment with 8 visualizations in the context of holistic evaluations, that considered two consequence matrices. One was developed for criteria with equal weights and the other for criteria with different weights. These were displayed in tables and bar charts. These visualizations represent decision problems applied to DMs who had to select the best alternative or to eliminate the worst one, depending on the case. With the results, it was possible to develop some hypotheses with the purpose of investigating the influence of participants' preferences on their ability to make choices, taking into account the probabilities of success and their preferences about the forms of visualizations (tables or bar graphs) and the type of problem (selection of the best alternative or elimination of the worst one).

The results of the hypothesis tests showed that participants presented similar probabilities of success in decision processes, independent of their preferences. However, more studies should be undertaken to confirm to confirm the phenomenon observed in descriptive analysis.

Behavioral studies have been developed to modulate the FITradeoff method and it DSS. In this context, the holistic evaluation of alternatives is performed in the FITradeoff DSS using graphical and tabular visualizations similar to those presented in the experiment. In addition, these visualizations can be applied to other methods in the MAVT context.

Hence, the experiment aims to test types of graphs and tables in order to investigate the cognitive effort demanded during the holistic evaluation and also to generate recommendations for DMs and analysts. During the interaction with the FITradeoff DSS, the analyst can use the Success-Based Decision Rule to support advising on whether to use or not to use a visualization to perform a holistic evaluation [22]. By obtaining knowledge about DMs' preferences and the influence on their choices, this study made a contribution by enabling the improvement of decision-making processes and future applications of holistic evaluations.

The use of these results should also be combined with the impact of the holistic evaluation in order to shorten the decomposition elicitation in FITradeoff. A set of simulation studies has been conducted in order to evaluate the use of holistic evaluation and decomposition elicitation in the FITradeoff method and other studies are also being conducted [45]. Previous results have shown that holistic evaluation can shorten the elicitation steps in FITradeoff. These results have also shown that choosing alternatives can be more efficient than eliminating alternatives so as to reduce the number of steps in the decomposition elicitation. Therefore, while there is a better probability of success by eliminating the worst alternative than by selecting the best alternative (Table 4), the latter is better for reducing the number of steps in the elicitation [45]. This brings another challenge for the analyst when advising the DM, since a tradeoff between the probability of success and reducing the number of steps should be made in choosing either to eliminate or to select alternatives.

As to suggestions for future lines of research, additional experiments with a different number of questions and other types of visualizations will be conducted. Moreover, analysis using the time spent to perform each decision tasks should be investigated. In addition, studies with neuroscience tools are being developed to investigate these two decision processes.

Acknowledgment. This work had partial support from the Brazilian Research Council (CNPq) [grant 308531/2015–9;312695/2020–9] and the Foundation of Support in Science and Technology of the State of Pernambuco (FACEPE) [APQ-0484-3.08/17].

References

1. Keeney, R.L., Raiffa, H.: Decisions with Multiple Objectives: Preferences, and Value Tradeoffs. Wiley, New York (1976)
2. Belton, V., Stewart, T.: Multiple Criteria Decision Analysis. Kluwer Academic Publishers, Dordrecht (2002)
3. Figueira, J., Greco, S., Ehrgott, M. (eds.) Multiple criteria decision analysis: state of the art surveys. Springer, Berlin (2005). https://doi.org/10.1007/b100605
4. De Almeida, A.T., Cavalcante, C.A.V., Alencar, M.H., Ferreira, R.J.P., de Almeida-Filho, A.T., Garcez, T.V.: Multicriteria and Multiobjective Models for Risk, Reliability and Maintenance Decision Analysis, vol. 231, Springer, Cham (2015). https://doi.org/10.1007/978-3-319-17969-8
5. de Almeida, A.T., Frej, E.A., Roselli, L.R.P.: Combining holistic and decomposition paradigms in preference modeling with the flexibility of FITradeoff. CEJOR **29**, 7–47 (2021)
6. de Almeida, A.T., Almeida, J.A., Costa, A.P.C.S., Almeida-Filho, A.T.: A new method for elicitation of criteria weights in additive models: flexible and interactive tradeoff. Eur. J. Oper. Res. **250**(1), 179–191 (2016)
7. Jacquet-Lagreze, E., Siskos, J.: Assessing a set of additive utility functions for multicriteria decision making, the UTA method. Eur. J. Oper. Res. **10**(2), 151–164 (1982)
8. Siskos, Y., Grigoroudis, E., Matsatsinis, N.F.: UTA methods. In: Greco, S., Ehrgott, M., Figueira, J. (eds.) Multiple Criteria Decision Analysis. International Series in Operations Research & Management Science, vol. 233. Springer, New York (2016). https://doi.org/10.1007/978-1-4939-3094-4
9. de Almeida, A.T., Frej, E.A., Roselli, L.R.P., Costa, A.P.C.S.: A summary on FITradeoff method with methodological and practical developments and future perspectives. Pesquisa Operacional **43**, e268356 (2023)

10. Czekajski, M., Wachowicz, T., Frej, E.A.: Exploring the combination of holistic evaluation and elicitation by decomposition in FITradeoff: prioritizing cultural tourism products in Poland. Pesquisa Operacional **43**, e263454 (2023)
11. Frej, E.A., Ekel, P., de Almeida, A.T.: A benefit-to-cost ratio based approach for portfolio selection under multiple criteria with incomplete preference information. Inf. Sci. **545**, 487–498 (2021)
12. Pergher, I., Frej, E.A., Roselli, L.R.P., de Almeida, A.T.: Integrating simulation and FITradeoff method for scheduling rules selection in job-shop production systems. Int. J. Prod. Econ. **227**, 107669 (2020)
13. Santos, I.M., Roselli, L.R.P., L., da Silva, A.L.G., Alencar, L.H.: A supplier selection model for a wholesaler and retailer company based on FITradeoff multicriteria method. Math. Prob. Eng. **2020**, 1–14 (2020)
14. Fossile, D.K., Frej, E.A., da Costa, S.E.G., de Lima, E.P., de Almeida, A.T.: Selecting the most viable renewable energy source for brazilian ports using the FITradeoff method. J. Clean. Prod. **260**, 121107 (2020)
15. Dell'Ovo, M., Oppio, A., Capolongo, S.: Modelling the spatial decision problem. Bridging the gap between theory and practice: SitHealth evaluation tool. In: Decision Support System for the Location of Healthcare Facilities. SpringerBriefs in Applied Sciences and Technology, pp. 81–112. Springer, Cham (2020). https://doi.org/10.1007/978-3-030-50173-0_4
16. Alvarez Carrillo, P.A., Roselli, L.R.P., Frej, E.A., et al.: Selecting an agricultural technology package based on the flexible and interactive tradeoff method. Ann. Oper. Res. **314**, 377–392 (2022). https://doi.org/10.1007/s10479-018-3020-y
17. Frej, E.A., Roselli, L.R.P., de Almeida, J.A., de Almeida, A.T.: A multicriteria decision model for supplier selection in a food industry based on FITradeoff method. Math. Prob. Eng. **2017**, 1–9 (2017)
18. de Almeida, A.T.: Processo de Decisão nas Organizações: Construindo Modelos de Decisão Multicritério, 2Ed. São Paulo: Editora Atlas (No prelo) (2020)
19. Korhonen, P., Wallenius, J.: Behavioral issues in MCDM: neglected research questions. In: Clímaco, J. (ed.) Multicriteria Analysis. Springer, Berlin, pp. 412–422 (1997). https://doi.org/10.1007/978-3-642-60667-0_39
20. Roselli, L.R.P., de Almeida, A.T.: Neuroscience behavioral studies for modula-tion of the FITradeoff Method. In: Morais, D.C., Fang, L. (eds.) Group Decision and Negotiation: Methodological and Practical Issues. GDN 2022. LNBIP, vol. 454, pp. 44–58. Springer, Cham (2022). https://doi.org/10.1007/978-3-031-07996-2_4
21. Eagleman, D.: The Brain: A Story of You. Pantheon Books, New York (2015)
22. Roselli, L.R.P., de Almeida, A.T.: The use of the success-based decision rule to support the holistic evaluation process in FITradeoff. Int. Trans. Oper. Res. **30**, 1299–1319 (2023)
23. Ferreira, E.B., de Vasconcelos, T.R.S., Roselli, L.R.P., de Almeida, A.T.: Behavioral studies for the use of visualization in holistic evaluation for multicriteria decision problems decision. In: Liu, S., Zaraté, P., Kamissoko, D., Linden, I., Papathanasiou, J. (eds.) Decision Support Systems XIII. Decision Support Systems in An Uncertain World: The Contribution of Digital Twins, ICDSST 2023, LNBIP, vol. 474, pp 265–276. Springer, Cham (2023). https://doi.org/10.1007/978-3-031-32534-2_19
24. Roselli, L.R.P., de Almeida, A.T.: Use of the Alpha-theta diagram as a decision neuroscience tool for analyzing holistic evaluation in decision making. Ann. Oper. Res. **290**, 1–23 (2022)
25. Reis Peixoto Roselli, L., de Almeida, A.T.: Analysis of graphical visualizations for multi-criteria decision making in FITradeoff method using a decision neuroscience experiment. In: Moreno-Jiménez, J., Linden, I., Dargam, F., Jayawickrama, U. (eds.) Decision Support Systems X: Cognitive Decision Support Systems and Technologies, ICDSST 2020, LNBP, vol. 384, pp. 30–42. Springer, Cham (2020). https://doi.org/10.1007/978-3-030-46224-6_3

26. Roselli, L.R.P., de Almeida, A.T.: Improvements in the FITradeoff decision support system for ranking order problematic based in a behavioral study with NeuroIS tools. In: Davis, F.D., Riedl, R., vom Brocke, J., Léger, PM., Randolph, A.B., Fischer, T. (eds.) Information Systems and Neuroscience. NeuroIS 2020. LNISO, vol. 43, pp. 121–132. Springer, Cham (2020). https://doi.org/10.1007/978-3-030-60073-0_14

27. Roselli, L.R.P., de Almeida, A.T., Frej, E.A.: Decision neuroscience for improving data visualization of decision support in the FITradeoff method. Oper. Res. Int. Journal **19**, 1–21 (2019)

28. Roselli, L.R.P., de Almeida, A.T.: Analyzing graphical visualization for multi-attribute decision making using EEG and eye-tracker. In NeuroPsychoEconomics Conference, Poster Section, Rome (2019)

29. Roselli, L.R.P., Frej, E.A., de Almeida, A.T.: Neuroscience experiment for graphical visualization in the FITradeoff decision support system. In: Chen, Y., Kersten, G., Vetschera, R., Xu, H. (eds.) Group Decision and Negotiation in an Uncertain World. GDN 2018, LNBIP, vol. 315, pp. 56–69. Springer, Cham (2018). https://doi.org/10.1007/978-3-319-92874-6_5

30. de Almeida, A.T., Roselli, L.R.P., Costa, A.P.C.S., Goncalves, J.M.S., Andrade, A.L.: Decision process improvement based on behavioral experiments of multi-attribute choices with graphical visualization. In: 16th Proceedings Society of NeuroEconomics, Philadelphia, USA (2018)

31. de Almeida, A.T., Roselli, L.R.P.: Visualization for decision support in FITradeoff method: exploring its evaluation with cognitive neuroscience. In: Linden, I., Liu, S., Colot, C. (eds.) Decision Support Systems VII. Data, Information and Knowledge Visualization in Decision Support Systems. ICDSST 2017, LNBIP, vol. 282, pp 61–73. Springer, Cham (2017). https://doi.org/10.1007/978-3-319-57487-5_5

32. da Silva, A.L.C.D.L., Costa, A.P.C.S., de Almeida, A.T.: Exploring cognitive aspects of FITradeoff method using neuroscience tools. Ann. Oper. Res. **312**(2), 1147–1169 (2022)

33. da Silva, A.L.C D.L., Costa, A.P.C.S., de Almeida, A.T.: Analysis of the cognitive aspects of the preference elicitation process in the compensatory context: a neuroscience experiment with FITradeoff. Int. Trans. Oper. Res. **31**, 2472–2503 (2024). https://doi.org/10.1111/itor.13210

34. Roselli, L.R.P., Pereira, L.D.S., da Silva, A.L.C.D.L., de Almeida, A.T., Morais, D.C., Costa, A.P.C.S.: Neuroscience experiment applied to investigate decision-maker behavior in the tradeoff elicitation procedure. Ann. Oper. Res. **289**(1), 67–84 (2020)

35. Carneiro de Lima da Silva, A.L., Cabral Seixas Costa, A.P.: FITradeoff decision support system: an exploratory study with neuroscience tools. In: Davis, F., Riedl, R., vom Brocke, J., Léger, PM., Randolph, A., Fischer, T. (eds.) Information Systems and Neuroscience, LNISO, vol. 32, pp 365–372. Springer, Cham (2020). https://doi.org/10.1007/978-3-030-28144-1_40

36. Frej, E.A., de Almeida, A.T.; Costa, A.P.C.S.: Using data visualization for ranking alternatives with partial information and interactive tradeoff elicitation. Oper. Res. **2019**, 1–23 (2019)

37. Kang, T.H.A., Frej, E.A., de Almeida, A.T.: Flexible and interactive tradeoff elicitation for multicriteria sorting problems. Asia Pacific J. Oper. Res. **37**, 2050020 (2020)

38. Engin, A., Vetschera, R.: Information representation in decision making: The impact of cognitive style and depletion effects. Decis. Support Syst. **103**, 94–103 (2017)

39. Nermend, K.: The implementation of cognitive neuroscience techniques for fatigue evaluation in participants of the decision-making process. In: Nermend, K., Łatuszyńska, M. (eds.) Neuroeconomic and Behavioral Aspects of Decision Making. Springer Proceedings in Business and Economics, pp 329–339. Springer, Cham (2017). https://doi.org/10.1007/978-3-319-62938-4_21

40. Özerol, G; Karasakal, E.: A parallel between regret theory and outranking methods for multicriteria decision making under imprecise information. Theor. Decis. **65**(1), 45–70 (2008)

41. Chuang, H., Lin, C., Chen, Y.: Exploring the triple reciprocity nature of organizational value cocreation behavior using multicriteria decision making analysis. Mathematical Problems in Engineering, pp. 1–15 (2015)
42. Trepel, C., Fox, C.R., Poldrack, R.: A. Prospect theory on the brain? Toward a cognitive neuroscience of decision under risk. Cogn. Brain Res. **23**(1), 34–50 (2005)
43. Barberis, N., Xiong, W.: What drives the disposition effect? An analysis of a long-standing preference-based explanation. J. Finance **64**(2), 751–784 (2009)
44. Wallenius, H., Wallenius, J.: Implications of world mega trends for MCDM research. In: Ben Amor, S., De Almeida, A., De Miranda, J., Aktas, E. (eds.). Advanced Studies in Multi-Criteria Decision Making. New York: Chapman and Hall/CRC, Series in Operations Research, 1st Ed, pp. 1–10 (2020)
45. de Almeida, A.T., Frej, E.A.: Simulation studies for evaluating the use of holistic evaluation and decomposition elicitation in the FITradeoff Method. Working Paper CDSID (2023)

A Comprehensive Examination of User Experience in AI-Based Symptom Checker Chatbots

Marta Campos Ferreira[1,2](✉) [ID], Maria Veloso[1], and João Manuel R. S. Tavares[1] [ID]

[1] Faculdade de Engenharia, Universidade Do Porto, R. Dr. Roberto Frias, 4200-465 Porto, Portugal
up202100658@edu.fe.up.pt, {mferreira,tavares}@fe.up.pt
[2] INESC-TEC, R. Dr. Roberto Frias, 4200-465 Porto, Portugal

Abstract. Recent advancements in digital technology have significantly impacted healthcare, with the rise of chatbots as a promising avenue for healthcare services. These chatbots aim to provide prevention, diagnosis, and treatment services, thereby reducing the workload on medical professionals. Despite this trend, limited research has explored the variables influencing user experiences in the design of healthcare chatbots. While the impact of visual representation within chatbot systems is recognized, existing studies have primarily focused on efficiency and accuracy, neglecting graphical interfaces and non-verbal visual communication tools. This research aims to delve into user experience aspects of symptom checker chatbots, including identity design, interface layout, and visual communication mechanisms. Data was collected through a comprehensive questionnaire involving three distinct chatbots (Healthily, Mediktor and Adele – a self-developed solution) and underwent meticulous analysis, yielding valuable insights to aid the decision process when designing effective chatbots for symptom checking.

Keywords: Artificial Intelligence · Chatbot · Healthcare · Interface Layout · Usability · Decision Process

1 Introduction

The World Health Organization's 2013 report highlighted a global shortage of healthcare professionals, projected to increase to 12.9 million by 2035 [1]. Primary care is particularly affected, with shortages worldwide. Europe faces a deficit of around one million healthcare workers due to professionals seeking better conditions [2]. The shortage impacts healthcare accessibility, disparities, waiting times, and emergency service usage. To address this, Artificial Intelligence (AI) technologies such as machine learning are increasingly being adopted to optimize the healthcare sector. Despite the proliferation of AI-based symptom checkers and chatbots, there is limited research on customer perceptions. This study aims to investigate the customer experience with symptom checker chatbots, by answering to the following research question: "What factors influence the customer experience with symptom checkers chatbots?".

S. P. Duarte et al. (Eds.): ICDSST 2024, LNBIP 506, pp. 98–108, 2024.
https://doi.org/10.1007/978-3-031-59376-5_8

The examination of the current literature highlights a dominant pattern among researchers, primarily focusing their efforts on exploring the practical aspects of chatbots, particularly emphasizing usability. Recognizing a distinctive gap in the research landscape, this study aims to address this void by shifting the focus towards the realm of hedonics. Specifically, the study aims to explore the interaction between interface design and the incorporation of anthropomorphism in chatbots, aiming to uncover how these elements collectively impact the enhancement of customer experiences. This intentional shift towards hedonics offers a chance to uncover fresh perspectives on the less examined yet crucial aspects of chatbot interactions, providing a more comprehensive understanding of the factors shaping user satisfaction and experience. To achieve this, three distinct AI-based symptom checker chatbots (Healthily, Mediktor and Adele – a self-developed solution) were compared, by 60 participants, through a comprehensive survey. The results provided valuable insights to assist the decision-making process of designing chatbot-based symptom checkers.

The remainder of this article is structured as follows: the next section presents the literature review. Section 3 details the methods used to conduct this study. Section 4 presents the main results and discussion. Section 5 summarizes the main findings.

2 Literature Review

The rise of online health information seekers has led to the proliferation of chatbot-based symptom checker (CSC) apps [3], offering immediate symptom evaluation and potential diagnoses. While these AI-powered tools provide efficient access to healthcare information, especially during challenges like the COVID-19 pandemic [3–6], comprehensive evaluations are lacking, emphasizing the necessity for thorough assessments prior to widespread healthcare integration.

While the current design of chatbots for healthcare places great importance on pragmatic user experience, research studies have also identified the positive effects of factors related to hedonic quality [7]. The chat interface not only pertains to usability but also contributes to user emotions by fostering specific atmospheres through design decisions affecting diverse elements, including the color of the background, overall arrangement of the layout, and the interaction with buttons. In contemporary chat applications designed for human interaction, the inclusion of audio clips and images within messages has become a common practice [8]. Lastly, non-verbal messages hold the potential for effective emotional sustenance; consequently, contemporary conversational exchanges incorporate an array of communication modalities encompassing images, videos, and auditory elements [8]. Primarily, these visual communication tools serve to shape perceptions of the user and foster the cultivation of positive sentiments and ideas.

The design considerations for chatbots also involve decisions about incorporating human-like attributes and characteristics, known as anthropomorphism. This approach aims to make conversational agents relatable and user-friendly. Studies have shown that humanness and anthropomorphism impact user experiences, influencing factors like trust and user perceptions [9]. However, excessive humanness can prompt discomfort and negative emotions, while an appropriate level of human resemblance enhances trust [10]. The choice of chatbot personality also plays a significant role, where tailoring it to the expected interaction is important. Empathetic medical chatbots have demonstrated positive effects on mental health, promoting adherence to prescribed remedies [11]. Addressing gender assignment to chatbots presents challenges due to the potential reinforcement of stereotypes. Research underscores the importance of considering gender implications in chatbot design and their impact on user perceptions and interactions [12].

3 Methods

This study centers on assessing the key determinants impacting customer experience concerning symptom checker chatbots, with a specific emphasis on interface design and the influence of anthropomorphism adoption. To achieve this, two chatbot applications, namely Healthily and Mediktor, were carefully selected. These chatbots were chosen due to their availability on mobile platforms and their capacity to serve as symptom checkers. The study aimed to encompass diverse chatbot features, including varying interface types, the provision of visual aids, and the presence of distinct personality traits. Additionally, a third chatbot was developed, called Adele, using the Microsoft Azure platform, which integrates personality traits such as a profile image, a designated name, and the incorporation of emojis.

The current study departs from a pragmatic stance to knowledge. Therefore, the approach is a mixed approach that uses both quantitative and qualitative data to achieve a comprehensive understanding of the customer experience with symptom checkers chatbots [13].

Quantitative data was collected through a comprehensive survey distributed to a user sample that had to access the three-symptom checkers chatbots. The survey covers various aspects, including interface perceptions, interactive elements, personality, overall satisfaction levels, and intentions to utilize or recommend the service in the future. To ensure wide participation, the survey was conducted online using Google Forms, and the collected data was analyzed using statistical software, namely Statistical Package for Social Science (SPSS) Version 26.

Qualitative data for this study was derived through open-ended questions included in the survey. This approach allows participants to provide detailed responses in their own words, offering insights and perspectives that might not be captured by closed-ended questions. By utilizing open questions, the research aims to tap into the richness of participants' experiences and viewpoints, thereby enhancing the depth and authenticity of the qualitative data collected. This method aligns with the objective of gaining a holistic understanding of the various dimensions of customer experiences with symptom checker chatbots, fostering a more comprehensive analysis and interpretation of the qualitative findings.

The survey consists of four sections. The primary goal of the initial section is to gather sociodemographic data. Within this segment, participants were asked about their proficiency levels with technology and whether they search for symptoms online. The final question in this section aimed to assess the respondent's familiarity with medical chatbots and to determine if they had engaged with chatbots previously.

In the second part of the survey, participants were provided with valuable hands-on experiences as they interacted with three distinct chatbots. These chatbots were introduced through links, allowing users to directly engage with the platforms. In addition to the links, participants were provided with user stories, which they could follow to effectively navigate and explore the functionalities of the chatbots. This approach not only enabled users to have a practical understanding of the chatbots but also allowed them to align their interactions with specific scenarios, enhancing the depth of their exploration. By combining direct interaction with user stories, Sects. 2, 3 and 4 aimed to gather comprehensive insights into the layout of the chatbots, integration of anthropomorphism, and overall user experience with the chatbots in a real-world context. On average the survey took approximately 30 min to answer depending on the chatbot interaction flow.

All selected chatbots were designed to support interactions in the English language.

Eligible participants, who were proficient in English, familiar with mobile applications, and aged between 18 and 50, were recruited with their informed consent. A total of 60 participants, comprising 34 males and 26 females, engaged in the research. Participants accessed the online survey through platforms like WhatsApp and Facebook. Participants were also encouraged to provide their insights through open-ended questions in the questionnaire, enriching the study's quantitative and qualitative aspect.

Healthily

Healthily, formerly known as Your.MD, is a renowned chatbot and digital health platform that offers personalized health information and guidance to users (see Fig. 1). Founded by Henrik Petterson in Norway in 2013, the Healthily chatbot is designed to simulate conversational interactions, providing symptom checking, health advice, and general health information. Powered by natural language processing and machine learning algorithms, the chatbot intelligently understands user queries and delivers relevant responses, showcasing the practical application of artificial intelligence [14].

The Healthily interface is meticulously crafted to prioritize user-friendliness and intuitiveness. It showcases a visual interface that seamlessly integrates text-based conversations for smooth interactions. Furthermore, the interface leverages well-designed visual elements, such as buttons and menus, to enhance the overall user experience and facilitate effortless navigation within the app. These visual components empower users to easily make selections and navigate through the interface, ensuring a user-friendly and engaging experience.

Mediktor

Mediktor was established in 2011 by Spanish founders Oscar García-Esquirol and Cristian Pascual [15]. It serves as a cutting-edge digital health platform and symptom assessment tool, harnessing the capabilities of artificial intelligence to guide users in evaluating their medical symptoms (see Fig. 2). Through the platform, users can effortlessly input their symptoms using natural language or by selecting from a curated list. Subsequently, Mediktor's advanced AI algorithms meticulously analyze the input, generating a comprehensive list of potential medical conditions that may correlate with the presented symptoms. This preliminary compilation aims to provide users with a foundational understanding to facilitate well-informed decisions concerning their health and potential courses of action.

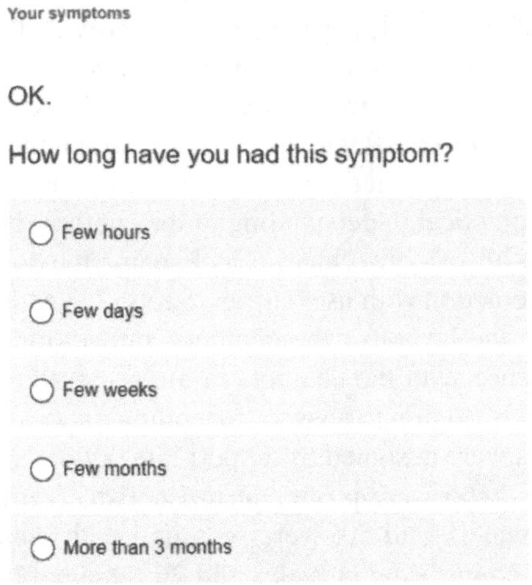

Your symptoms

OK.

How long have you had this symptom?

○ Few hours

○ Few days

○ Few weeks

○ Few months

○ More than 3 months

Fig. 1. Healthily chatbot interface

In conjunction with its sophisticated functionality, Mediktor boasts an interface that prioritizes user-friendliness and intuitive navigation. Characterized by tranquil and neutral color palettes, the interface establishes a serene and reassuring atmosphere. Thoughtfully designed, it incorporates visual aids that empower users to vividly communicate and articulate their discomfort or symptoms. By integrating images and visual cues, the platform enhances users' ability to precisely convey the nature and location of their afflictions, thereby refining the accuracy of the symptom assessment process. The combination of neutral tones and illustrative elements not only creates an aesthetically pleasing interface but also encourages clear and comprehensive communication. This, in turn, empowers users to engage with the platform more effectively.

Adele

The development of a third chatbot was essential to meet the evolving needs of users and enhance their interaction with the interface. Unlike the previous two chatbots, the developed chatbot, called Adele, introduce the element of free text entry, allowing users to express their queries and concerns in a more natural and unrestricted manner (see Fig. 3). This feature eliminates the constraints of predefined options, enabling the chatbot to understand and respond to a wider range of user inputs. Furthermore, the incorporation of affective communication empowers the chatbot to recognize and respond to users' emotions, fostering a more empathetic and human-like interaction. By infusing personality traits into the chatbot, it becomes more relatable and engaging, establishing a stronger connection with users, and promoting longer and more satisfying conversations.

Additionally, by including accessibility features such as the option to increase font size and the ability to speak instead of type, the chatbot becomes more inclusive, catering to individuals with visual impairments or those who prefer voice input. These improvements collectively aim to improve the user experience, making it more intuitive, personalized, and accessible, ultimately leading to enhanced satisfaction and effective communication with the chatbot.

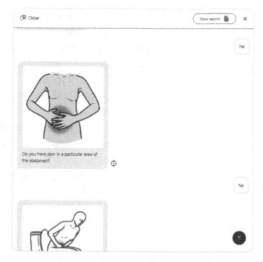

Fig. 2. Mediktor chatbot interface

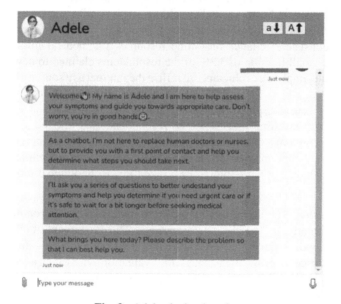

Fig. 3. Adele chatbot interface

4 Results and Discussion

Sample Characterization A total of 60 participants engaged in this study. Regarding the demographic characteristics of the sample, out of the 60 participants, 26 identified as female, accounting for 43.3% of the total, while 34 identified as male, representing 56.7%. The average age of the participants was 27.3 years, with a standard deviation of 4.7. Most participants (63.3%) were above the age of 27. The youngest participant was

18 years old, while the oldest participant was 41 years old. Participants were also asked to provide information about their Education Level, indicating the highest level of education they had completed. Among the participants, the majority, 29 in total (48.3%), reported having obtained a bachelor's degree. Additionally, 14 participants (23.3%) indicated having completed a master's degree, and another 14 participants (23.3%) reported having a high school degree. Two participants stated that they had completed their PhD, while one participant chose not to disclose their education level.

Regarding the proficiency of users with technology, most participants, comprising 51%, fall into the intermediate proficiency category. A small percentage, 3.3%, are classified as beginners in terms of technology proficiency. On the other hand, a significant proportion of participants, accounting for 45%, demonstrate advanced proficiency in utilizing technology. This distribution provides insights into the participants' technological skills and their readiness to engage with technology-driven solutions.

Participants were asked about the frequency with which they search for information about their symptoms online, and the majority, comprising 53.3% of the respondents, occasionally search for information online. This suggests that a significant portion of the population turns to the internet as a resource to gather information about their symptoms from time to time. Additionally, 21.7% of the respondents stated that they rarely search for symptoms online, indicating that they seldom rely on online sources for information. Similarly, another 21.7% mentioned that they frequently search for symptoms online, suggesting a consistent reliance on online resources for medical information. Interestingly, only a small fraction of 3.3% of the respondents claimed to never search their symptoms online, implying a reluctance to utilize the internet as a source of health-related information.

Participants were additionally queried regarding their prior experience with symptom checker chatbots, unveiling that 21.7% of respondents had utilized such chatbots to evaluate their symptoms. On the other hand, most participants, compromising 78.3%, have not used a symptom checker chatbot. This suggest that a significant portion of the respondents have not yet explored or utilized this technological tool for symptom evaluation.

Chatbot Evaluation The initial inquiry aimed to understand users' opinions regarding the visual presentation of the chatbots' interfaces. The assessment of chatbot interface attributes was conducted using a Likert scale ranging from 1 to 5 (1 – strongly disagree, to 5 – strongly agree). Across all instances, the evaluations yielded an average exceeding 3, signifying favorable assessments of the interface attributes in every scenario. The main results are shown in Table 1.

Overall, the comprehensive evaluation of the chatbots' interfaces reveals that chatbot Mediktor consistently received more positive ratings across all dimensions assessed. Participants found chatbot Mediktor's interface to be visually appealing, easy to navigate, and responsive, as evidenced by its higher mean scores in these areas compared to chatbot Healthilty and chatbot Adele. This pattern of results highlights the favorable impression that chatbot Mediktor's interface made on users. Its design and functionality seem to have resonated with participants, indicating a higher level of satisfaction and effectiveness in

Table 1. Assessement of chatbot interfaces

Characteristic	Healthily	Mediktor	Adele
I find the interface visually appealing	$\mu = 3.33$ $\sigma_X = 1.068$	$\mu = 3.97$ $\sigma_X = 1.178$	$\mu = 3.18$ $\sigma_X = 1.372$
The interface of the chatbot is intuitive	$\mu = 3.82$ $\sigma_X = 1.033$	$\mu = 4.15$ $\sigma_X = 0.840$	$\mu = 3.62$ $\sigma_X = 1.010$
The interface of the chatbot improved my navigation	$\mu = 3.62$ $\sigma_X = 1.121$	$\mu = 4.08$ $\sigma_X = 0.889$	$\mu = 3.75$ $\sigma_X = 1.083$
The interface of the chatbot facilitated understanding and following the prompts	$\mu = 3.78$ $\sigma_X = 1.043$	$\mu = 4.22$ $\sigma_X = 0.783$	$\mu = 3.92$ $\sigma_X = 1.046$
The interface allowed me to input my systems easily	$\mu = 3.83$ $\sigma_X = 1.167$	$\mu = 4.32$ $\sigma_X = 0.892$	$\mu = 3.92$ $\sigma_X = 1.062$
The interface was responsive	$\mu = 3.95$ $\sigma_X = 0.946$	$\mu = 4.33$ $\sigma_X = 0.933$	$\mu = 3.88$ $\sigma_X = 1.277$
I enjoyed using the chatbot	$\mu = 3.45$ $\sigma_X = 1.213$	$\mu = 4.10$ $\sigma_X = 0.877$	$\mu = 3.55$ $\sigma_X = 1.141$
I would use chatbot again	$\mu = 3.25$ $\sigma_X = 1.271$	$\mu = 3.93$ $\sigma_X = 1.087$	$\mu = 3.57$ $\sigma_X = 1.155$

providing a positive user experience. These findings underscore the importance of a well-designed interface in enhancing user interactions and perceptions, positioning chatbot Mediktor as a noteworthy example in interface design among the evaluated chatbots.

Additionally, participants were asked about the preference of interface to interact with. The results indicate that among the participants, 63.63% preferred a conversational interface for the chatbot. This type of interface allows for more natural and interactive conversations with the chatbot. On the other hand, 36.37% of participants favored a traditional interface, which typically involves structured interactions and predefined options. These results highlight the majority preference for a conversational interface, suggesting a preference for more dynamic and human-like interactions with the chatbot.

In the concluding phase, participants were questioned about their preference for either a chatbot with a personality or one devoid of personality. The results indicate that among the participants, 23% responded with "it makes no difference" when asked about their preference for interacting with a chatbot with or without a personality. Additionally, 12% of participants expressed a preference for a chatbot that does not have a personality. However, most participants, 65.0%, indicated a preference for interacting with a chatbot that has a personality. These findings highlight the significance of incorporating a personality in chatbots, as it appears to be favored by a significant portion of users, potentially enhancing the overall user experience and engagement.

Finally, participants' experiences with the chatbots were generally positive, as indicated by the fact that the mean ratings for all three chatbots exceeded the midpoint of the scale (3). Notably, chatbot Mediktor emerged as the most favorably received, boasting a significantly higher mean rating above 4, suggesting that the experience with chatbot

Mediktor was superior in comparison to chatbots Healthily and Adele. This suggests that, while participants reported having a positive experience and found all three chatbots to be acceptable for potential reuse, chatbot Mediktor left a particularly positive impression, outshining its counterparts in terms of user satisfaction.

During the monitoring of the interaction between participants and the chatbots, it was possible to collect comments that participants provided, such as:

"The interaction with chatbot Healthily felt very mechanical and visually robotic. It was a bit of a hassle having to type out all the information every time".

"Chatbot Mediktor had a visually engaging interface that resembled texting a doctor friend. There was minimal typing involved, as only initial information was required. The interaction involved checking off answers like responding to a nurse's questions".

"Chatting with chatbot Adele was like talking to a nurse. However, it still required typing out all the information".

5 Conclusion

The fundamental objective of this research was to gain a comprehensive understanding of the customer experience when interacting with symptom checker chatbots, with a specific focus on two key aspects: the interface design and the integration of personality traits. Delving into these dimensions aimed to shed light on the intricate dynamics that shape users' perceptions and interactions with these chatbots, unraveling the pivotal roles that design aesthetics and the infusion of human-like traits play in influencing user satisfaction, and customer experience.

The findings from the study allowed for the conclusion that an optimized user interface, coupled with the integration of personality traits, significantly impacts the customer experience. The results provided compelling evidence that a thoughtfully designed interface, tailored to user preferences, plays a pivotal role in shaping positive interactions. Furthermore, the incorporation of personality traits into the chatbot interaction added an element of relatability and engagement, enhancing the overall user experience. These insights underscore the crucial relationship between user-centric design principles and the infusion of human-like attributes, affirming their collective influence on promoting a satisfying and engaging customer journey.

In summary, several considerations can be drawn from the results to assist the decision process of designing chatbot-based symptom checkers, namely:

- Conversational Interface: The chatbot interface should closely emulate human conversations, ensuring interactions are intuitive and natural for users.
- Identity: Incorporating anthropomorphism by giving the chatbot a name, profile photo, and using emotionally resonant language enhances trust and familiarity, thereby improving the overall user experience.
- Diverse Symptom Input Methods: To cater to user preferences, the chatbot should accommodate symptom input through text, speech, or pre-defined buttons.
- Visual Support: Integrating visual communication tools, such as body maps, allows users to pinpoint specific areas of discomfort, enhancing accuracy in symptom reporting.

- Personalized Interfaces: Offering users the ability to customize background colors and even play background music tailors the experience to individual preferences.
- Accessibility Features: To ensure inclusivity, the chatbot should include options to enlarge font size for visually impaired users and provide text-to-speech functionality for those who may require auditory support.

Future research endeavors should consider exploring further into the individual dimensions of both interface design and personality traits to ascertain their nuanced influences on customer experience. Additionally, investigating the interrelationships between these two factors could provide insights into how they jointly impact user satisfaction. The multifaceted nature of customer experience with symptom checker chatbots necessitates a holistic approach that considers both interface design and personality implementation. This study serves as a foundation for further inquiries, guiding the refinement of strategies to enhance user satisfaction and the effectiveness of these digital healthcare tools.

References

1. Ceney, A., Tolond, S., Glowinski, A., Marks, B., Swift, S., Palser, T.: "Accuracy of online symptom checkers and the potential impact on service utilisation", (in eng). PLoS ONE **16**(7), e0254088 (2021). https://doi.org/10.1371/journal.pone.0254088
2. Put the horse before the cart: Investing in health requires investing in health workforce. https://health.ec.europa.eu/other-pages/basic-page/health-eu-newsletter-250-focus_en#:~:text=There%20is%20an%20estimated%20shortage,leaving%20other%20countries%20with%20shortages. Accessed 12 Apr 2023
3. Espinoza, J., Crown, K., Kulkarni, O.: A guide to chatbots for COVID-19 screening at pediatric health care facilities. JMIR Public Health Surveill. **6**(2), e18808 (2020)
4. Morse, K.E., Ostberg, N.P., Jones, V.G., Chan, A.S.: Use characteristics and triage acuity of a digital symptom checker in a large integrated health system: population-based descriptive study," (in eng). J. Med. Internet Res. **22**(11), e20549 (2020). https://doi.org/10.2196/20549
5. Martin, A., et al.: An artificial intelligence-based first-line defence against COVID-19: digitally screening citizens for risks via a chatbot. Sci. Rep. **10**(1), 1–7 (2020)
6. Almalki, M.: Perceived utilities of COVID-19 related chatbots in Saudi Arabia: a cross-sectional study. Acta Informatica Medica **28**(3), 218 (2020)
7. Denecke, K., May, R.: Usability assessment of conversational agents in healthcare: a literature review, pp. 169–173 (2022)
8. Følstad, A., Brandtzæg, P.B.: Chatbots and the new world of HCI. Interactions 24(4), 38–42 (2017)
9. McDuff, D., Czerwinski, M.: Designing emotionally sentient agents. Commun. ACM **61**, 74–83 (2018)
10. Meyer, J., Miller, C., Hancock, P., De Visser, E.J., Dorneich, M.: Politeness in machine-human and human-human interaction. Proc. Hum. Factors Ergon. Soc. **60**, 279–283 (2016)
11. Félix, B., Ribeiro, J.: Understanding People's Expectations When Designing a Chatbot for Cancer Patients, vol. 13171. Springer, Cham (2022)
12. Brahnam, S., De Angeli, A.: Gender affordances of conversational agents. Interact. Comput. **24**, 139–153 (2012)
13. Creswell, J.W., Creswell, J.D.: Research Design: Qualitative, Quantitative, and Mixed Methods Approaches. Sage publications (2017)

14. Davenport, T.H., Ronanki, R.: Artificial intelligence for the real world. Harv. Bus. Rev.. Bus. Rev. **96**(1), 108–116 (2018)
15. Barriga, E.M., Ferrer, I.P., Sánchez, M.S., Baranera, M.M., Utset, J.M.: Experiencia de Mediktor®: un nuevo evaluador de síntomas basado en inteligencia artificial para pacientes atendidos en el servicio de urgencias. Emergencias: Revista de la Sociedad Española de Medicina de Urgencias y Emergencias **29**(6), 391–396 (2017)

Framework for Understanding Consumer Perceptions and Attitudes to Support Decisions on Cultured Meat: A Theoretical Approach and Future Directions

Guoste Pivoraite[1]([✉]), Shaofeng Liu[1], Saeyeon Roh[1], and Guoqing Zhao[2]

[1] Plymouth Business School, University of Plymouth, Plymouth 4 8AA, UK
guoste.pivoraite@plymouth.ac.uk
[2] School of Management, Swansea University, Swansea SA1 8EN, UK

Abstract. This paper investigated consumer perceptions and attitudes for decision making in Cultured Meat (CM), driven by the growing interest in innovative food products. The motivation stemmed from the anticipated challenges in consumer acceptance of CM, a novel alternative to traditional meat production. The research objective included to identify key factors influencing consumer behaviour in the context of the novel food product. The Systematic Literature Review methodically explored and synthesised existing research, giving insights to the factors affecting consumer perceptions and attitudes towards decisions on CM. Then, a tailored conceptual framework, the Cultured Meat Attitude and Perception Assessment (CAPA), has been developed to address the identified gaps and limitations in understanding consumer perceptions and attitudes. The results highlighted the complex and multidimensional nature of consumer attitudes, emphasising the role of knowledge (awareness, comprehension, familiarity), perception (disgust, neophobia, curiosity, fear, trust), and external factors (ethical issues, social factors, product attributes, information influence, perceived exclusivity, regulatory considerations) that could be used by decision makers such as food innovators and marketers. The CAPA framework integrated these factors to offer a holistic perspective on consumer behaviour, overcoming the limitations of existing work and offering insights to the decision makers in the industry.

Keywords: Consumer Behaviour · Decision Factors · Food Innovation · Cultured Meat

1 Introduction

The global landscape of food production, driven by many decision factors such as population growth and rising incomes, stands on the brink of significant transformation (María Ignacia Rodríguez et al., 2021). Over the past decade, heightened scrutiny of the environmental, ethical, and health implications of the global livestock industry has led to a critical re-evaluation of food value chain sectors (Stephens et al., 2018; Pakseresht et al., 2022). Livestock production, contributing to approximately 80% of greenhouse

S. P. Duarte et al. (Eds.): ICDSST 2024, LNBIP 506, pp. 109–125, 2024.
https://doi.org/10.1007/978-3-031-59376-5_9

gas emissions within food supply chains, poses a substantial risk to climate change mitigation (María Ignacia Rodríguez et al., 2021). Responding to these challenges, a groundbreaking solution has emerged: Cultured Meat (CM). This transformative technology signifies a paradigm shift in meat production, enabling the cultivation of meat products outside live animals through the utilisation of animal stem cells and tissue engineering techniques (Rischer et al., 2020). CM technology facilitates the creation of biologically equivalent products to those derived from traditional livestock farming, with the potential to reduce or eliminate the need for live animals, which means that it offers a solution to reduce the environmental pressure caused by livestock farming, including deforestation, water pollution, and biodiversity loss, by significantly reducing the land and water requirements for meat production (Wilks and Phillips, 2017). Moreover, CM aims to replicate the sensory attributes of animal-sourced counterparts while matching their nutritional characteristics, therefore providing consumers with a sustainable and ethically viable alternative to conventionally produced meat (de Oliveira Padilha et al., 2022).

Despite its prospects, large-scale production and commercialisation of CM are still in their infancy (Pakseresht et al., 2022). Various barriers, including technological concerns such as the development of large-scale bioreactors and efficient growth media, hinder its industrial-scale production (Onwezen et al., 2021). The technological viability of CM products also faces challenges due to multiple decision criteria, for example, high production costs, impeding competitive pricing (Fernandes et al., 2022a, 2022b). Consumer perspectives represent another critical barrier to novel food acceptance, with studies indicating a wide spectrum of views, from low to high acceptance rates (Onwezen et al., 2021; Pakseresht et al., 2022; Siddiqui et al., 2022). This underscores the need for further exploration and understanding of decision factors such as consumer attitudes towards CM products (Ruzgys and Pickering, 2020; Tomiyama et al., 2020; Weinrich et al., 2020).

This paper explores the intricacies of consumer decision-making for novel food products, specifically focusing on CM and various decision factors linked to CM to understand consumer perceptions and attitudes during the pre-commercialisation phase. The study aims to unravel relationships influencing these perceptions and attitudes, with the goal of establishing a conceptual framework to support food innovators and marketers for their decisions. Through a systematic literature review, the primary objective is to identify specific decision factors. Contributions encompass a comprehensive analysis of existing work on the factors impacting consumer perceptions and attitudes towards CM, providing insights into the current state of knowledge. The conceptual framework serves as a valuable tool for researchers, policymakers, industry stakeholders, and decision-makers looking to understand and enhance the consumer decision-making journey. Additionally, the study lays the foundation for future research, uncovering the complex interplay of decision factors influencing consumer attitudes toward pre-commercialized food innovations like CM.

2 Methodology - Systematic Literature Review

This paper employed the Systematic Literature Review (SLR) methodology, a comprehensive approach grounded in established literature and academic guidance (Denyer and Tranfield, 2009; Booth et al., 2012). This methodology was chosen for its structured nature, offering advantages over traditional literature reviews by providing a systematic approach to synthesizing existing research.

Firstly, the SLR process involved formulating clear and well-defined research questions. In this case, the questions formulated were: 1) What are the internal and external decision factors that influence consumers' attitudes towards cultured meats and, subsequently, their intention to purchase these products? 2) How do these internal and external factors interact with consumers' attitudes, ultimately shaping their intention to purchase cultured meat?

Secondly, the identification of relevant research papers required a comprehensive search strategy. Reputable databases, including Scopus, Web of Science, and PubMed, were selected based on their relevance and reputation. The query, combining keywords reflecting the research objectives, guided the selection of databases. The overall query was composed by combining keywords, Boolean operators, special symbols, and grouping similar words: (cellular agriculture OR lab grown meat OR artificial meat OR cell cultured meat OR clean meat OR cultivated meat OR Cultured meat OR in vitro meat OR animal free meat OR cell based meat OR craft meat OR cruelty free meat OR factory grown meat OR fake meat OR meat 2.0 OR pure meat OR safe meat OR schmeat OR slaughter free meat OR synthetic meat) AND (View* OR attitude* OR intent* OR perce* OR opinion* OR willing* OR accept* OR adopt* OR behav*).

Then, the systematic approach to paper selection and evaluation was implemented, involving explicit inclusion and exclusion criteria (as shown in Table 1) aligned with research questions (Booth et al., 2012). These criteria encompassed the theoretical foundation, research methods, data collection, analysis, and overall paper quality. This rigorous selection process minimized biases and ensured the inclusion of the most relevant and methodologically sound studies.

Following this, the overall process of the literature selection is illustrated in Fig. 1. After identifying papers using the mentioned queries from the relevant databases, the inclusion and exclusion criteria were applied, duplicates removed, the papers were screened by title and abstract, and then based on full-text. After adding additional relevant papers, 67 papers formed the final collection of literature and included in the analysis.

Following paper selection, the data extraction and synthesis stage systematically extracted key information from each paper, aiming to identify common themes, patterns, and discrepancies across the selected papers. Synthesis contributed to a nuanced understanding of the decision factors shaping consumer attitudes towards Cultured Meat.

The synthesis of findings addressed the research questions, offering insights into commonalities, contradictions, and gaps in the existing literature. The presentation of the last step, the development of the conceptual framework, will be detailed in the next section.

Table 1. SLR inclusion and exclusion criteria

Criteria	Inclusion	Exclusion
Identification stage		
Availability	Full-text available	No full-text available
Peer-review	Peer-reviewed	Not peer-reviewed
Type of publication	Journal articles	Conference proceedings, book chapters, review articles, etc.
Timeframe	2008–2023	Before 2008
Language	English Language	Non-English
Relevant subject area	Social Sciences	Hard Sciences (Biological Sciences, Medicine, Chemistry, etc.)
Screening stage		
Type of study	Empirical and Theoretical studies	discussion papers, overviews, opinion papers
Study Focus	Studies focused on consumer behaviour	Technical studies and papers not focusing on consumer behaviour
Relevance	Studies about cultured meat	- Studies focused on other meat alternatives (plant-based alternatives, insect-based substitutes, etc.) - Studies focused on other Cellular Agriculture products

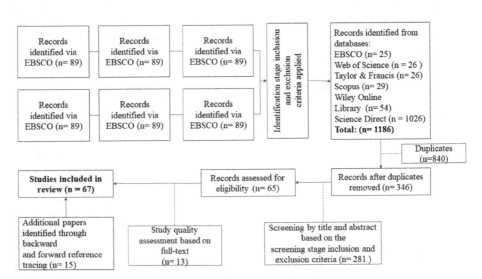

Fig. 1. Selection of papers flowchart

3 Key Findings from Systematic Literature Review

The findings from the SLR are organized into three key themes: internal decision factors (i.e. factors related to the consumers themselves), external decision factors (i.e. factors related to external environment), and links among different decision factors.

3.1 Internal Decision Factors

In exploring consumer decisions on CM, the SLR revealed that internal factors such as knowledge, perception, and personal elements play an important role in shaping consumer attitudes. As such, this section examines these internal aspects, providing insights into the dynamics influencing consumer decision-making regarding CM.

Knowledge. Consumer decision-making in terms of CM was significantly influenced by their own knowledge, comprising awareness, familiarity, and comprehension. Baum et al. (2022) found that prior knowledge had a limited impact on altering consumer acceptance, suggesting that awareness alone didn't drive attitude change. Hwang et al. (2020), however, reported a positive relationship between prior knowledge and consumer willingness to purchase CM, indicating that increased understanding enhances acceptance. Gousset et al. (2022), on the other hand, revealed that prior awareness did not significantly impact consumer overall feelings toward CM as well. It is notable, that these contrasting findings highlight the complexity of the relationship between prior knowledge and attitude.

Meanwhile familiarity, often intertwined with awareness, was recognised as a significant dimension of consumer knowledge too. Giacalone and Jaeger (2023) emphasised its importance however, Baum et al. (2022) reported that familiarity with meat substitutes did not significantly impact acceptance change, suggesting other factors like consumer effectiveness and message framing were more influential.

In term of comprehension, it pertained to consumers' understanding about CM and its production processes. Shan et al. (2022) found that higher levels of knowledge reduced susceptibility to framing effects, indicating comprehension acted as a safeguard. However, Li et al. (2023) found that comprehensive understanding alone may not positively influence attitudes, hinting at potential consumer resistance.

The nuanced relationship between these knowledge dimensions underscored the complexity of consumer understanding about CM, calling for further research to explore the interplay between different knowledge dimensions.

Perception. Perception, encompassing cognitive and emotional processes, played a role in shaping consumer attitudes towards novel food technologies like CM. Disgust consistently emerged as a crucial factor due to CM's perceived artificiality (Siegrist and Hartmann, 2020; Rosenfeld and Tomiyama, 2022). Food neophobia, fear of trying new foods, consistently influenced CM attitudes, impacting views on safety (Krings et al., 2022) while curiosity emerged as a significant driver for trying CM due to its innovative nature (Liu et al., 2021; Hocquette et al., 2022). In addition, the complexity of factors influencing consumer perception extended to fear, uncertainty, liking, and scepticism too. Some expressed liking driven by perceived advantages, while others expressed scepticism and concerns (Wilks et al., 2019; Hamlin et al., 2022; Giacalone and Jaeger, 2023), highlighting the complex nature of consumer perceptions.

Personal Factors. Dietary preferences, age, gender, education, income, and cultural context played crucial roles in shaping consumer attitudes toward CM. For example, meat eaters showed higher intentions to try CM (Liu et al., 2021), and cultural background significantly influenced consumer attitudes, as seen in vegetarian preferences (Arora et al., 2020). Age and cultural context could influence openness and acceptance as well (Dupont and Fiebelkorn, 2020; Liu et al., 2021). In terms of gender differences, they played an essential role, with men generally exhibiting greater willingness to try CM than women (Da Silva and da Cunha, 2022). Education correlated with positive attitudes (Zhang et al., 2020), but highly educated individuals expressed concerns related to economic disruptions (Tsvakirai et al., 2023). Looking at income levels, this factor impacted consumer attitudes, with higher income associated with a greater willingness to pay for cultured meat (Zhang et al., 2022). In addition, cultural context significantly shaped consumer attitudes too (Bekker et al., 2017; Siegrist and Hartmann, 2020).

3.2 External Decision Factors

Shifting the focus outward, external factors, explored subsequently, contributed additional layers to the intricate framework shaping consumer attitudes and impacting decision-making in the context of CM. SLR findings indicated that the dynamics of consumer attitudes toward CM were connected to these external elements, reaching beyond individual cognitive processes.

Ethical Issues Ethical concerns surrounding CM comprised environmental sustainability, animal welfare, food security, and social considerations, collectively shaping consumer attitudes. While sustainability consistently emerged as a driving force, nuanced findings revealed the complex interplay of factors influencing acceptance (Palmieri et al., 2020; Specht et al., 2020; da Silva and da Cunha, 2022). Ethical concerns for animal welfare remained strong across the literature, emphasising the enduring influence of more humane alternatives (Wilks and Phillips, 2017; Palmieri et al., 2020; Ruzgys and Pickering, 2020; Liu et al., 2021; Verbeke et al., 2021; Gousset et al., 2022). Food security also played a notable role, particularly in regions facing challenges. Additionally, social considerations highlighted mixed views on the impact of cultured meat, necessitating further exploration of its broader societal consequences (de Oliveira et al., 2022; Dean et al., 2023).

Product Attributes. Consumer perceptions of CM were influenced by healthiness, safety, nutrition, naturalness, sensory properties, and price. Healthiness was positively associated with acceptance (Gómez-Luciano et al., 2019; Specht et al., 2020; Zhang et al., 2020; de Oliveira et al., 2021; Da Silva and da Cunha, 2022). Safety was considered a critical factor, with controlled production environments enhancing perceived safety (Liu et al., 2021). Naturalness, a consistent barrier, required careful management of diverse perceptions (Ruzgys and Pickering, 2020; Giacalone and Jaeger, 2023). Sensory properties, particularly taste and texture, significantly influenced acceptance, emphasising the need to align CM with familiar expectations (Mancini and Antonioli, 2019; Zhang et al., 2020; Dean et al., 2023). Price sensitivity posed challenges, with concerns about high costs prevalent (Verbeke et al., 2015a, 2015b; Wilks and Phillips, 2017; de Oliveira et al., 2022).

Information Influence. Information, nomenclature, and labelling was another set of elements that impacted consumer perceptions of CM. Detailed information and visual imagery may not uniformly sway consumer evaluations (Baum et al., 2023) however, message framing positively influenced willingness to pay (Zhang et al., 2022). Combining appeals and diverse information types showed to be effective as well (Septianto et al., 2023a, 2023b; Piochi et al., 2022). In addition, nomenclature significantly shaped consumer behaviour, with careful selection essential for positive responses (Califano et al., 2023; Li et al., 2023; Bryant and Barnett, 2019). Furthermore, labelling and packaging, such as green packaging and specific labels, influenced consumer preferences and behavioural intentions (Asioli et al., 2022a, 2022b; Dupont et al., 2022; Krings et al., 2022).

Social Influence. Limited research explored social factors influencing consumer perceptions of CM. Cultural factors, peer opinions on social media, and social settings played roles in shaping perceptions and acceptance (Chong et al., 2022; Leong, 2022; Motoki et al., 2022). Exposure to lab-grown meat information through social media influencers proved to not significantly impact acceptance while social image motivations varied (Chong et al., 2022). Peer opinions on social media shaped public perceptions and decisions, emphasising the importance of congruence between elite and lay perspectives (Leong, 2022). Additionally, social situations, such as dining with friends, influenced the expected acceptance of cultured meat (Motoki et al., 2022).

While research on social influence concerning cultured meat appeared to be limited, these studies offered valuable insights into consumer attitudes and behaviours. Cultural factors, peer opinions on social media, and social settings all played roles in shaping perceptions and acceptance. Further exploration of these factors within the context of CM may be beneficial to develop a more comprehensive understanding of their impact.

Perceived Exclusivity. Perceived exclusivity, encompassing elements like luxury and scarcity, gained prominence in recent studies examining consumer attitudes toward CM. Arango, Chaudhury, and Septianto's (2023) study on demand-based scarcity appeals provided valuable insights into a marketing strategy that promoted cultured meat by leveraging scarcity to create a sense of limited availability. This approach not only mitigated perceptions of risk but also instilled a feeling of exclusivity among consumers, aligning with the broader literature on scarcity appeals. Septianto et al. (2023a, 2023b) delved into the role of perceived luxuriousness as a mediating factor in consumers' willingness to try clean meat products. Their study revealed that visual representations conveying an artistic and luxurious aura positively influenced consumer attitudes, underscoring the impact of aesthetics in shaping perceptions. However, it is important to acknowledge that while these studies shed light on the role of perceived exclusivity, the broader context of luxury and scarcity in consumer behaviour and its connection to cultured meat requires further exploration.

Regulatory Considerations. Regulatory considerations emerged as another aspect of consumer attitudes toward CM. Zhang, Li and Bai's (2020) study conducted in urban areas of China highlighted the influence of government regulation of food safety on consumer acceptance. Respondents who expressed higher satisfaction with government food safety regulations were more likely to accept cultured meat, underscoring the role of regulatory trust in consumer acceptance. Ryynanen and Toivanen's (2023) analysis of online comments in Finnish media discussions revealed diverse views on the role of the state and decision-making processes in shaping the future of cultured meat. While some individuals emphasised individual choice, others favoured democratic decision-making and policy interventions, suggesting a need for balanced regulatory approaches. Specht et al. (2020) explored social media discourse surrounding cultured meat discussions, with regulatory discussions featuring prominently. Conversations highlighted the need for transparent regulations to ensure safety, quality, and consumer confidence in cultured meat products. However, these studies primarily acknowledged the role of regulations without providing extensive details on specific regulatory policies, indicating a need for further research in this area.

3.3 Links Between Internal and External Factors

In examining the interplay of various internal and external factors, the study revealed relationships crucial for understanding the complexity of consumer attitudes towards CM such as the one between consumer knowledge and the perception of CM. Baum et al. (2022) found that prior knowledge had a limited impact on altering consumer acceptance, suggesting that mere awareness might not have been the primary driver of attitude change. Conversely, Hwang et al. (2020) reported a positive relationship between prior knowledge and consumer willingness to purchase cultured meat, highlighting the nuanced nature of the knowledge-perception relationship.

The nexus of consumer perception, attitudes, and knowledge emerged as pivotal in the context of CM too. Factors within perception, such as neophobia, fear, disgust, and curiosity, played key roles in shaping attitudes towards these novel food technologies. Strategic messaging and framing moderated negative emotions, influencing the perception-attitude relationship. Conversely, curiosity fostered open-mindedness, contributing to more favourable attitudes (Gómez-Luciano et al., 2019).

External factors, including ethical concerns, product attributes, information influence, social influence, perceived exclusivity, and regulatory considerations, collectively shaped consumer attitudes. Ethical issues, such as environmental sustainability and animal welfare, consistently influenced attitudes (Dean et al., 2023; Weinrich et al., 2020). Product attributes, including healthiness and naturalness, impacted consumer attitudes, with these perceptions contributing to overall acceptance (Gómez-Luciano et al., 2019; Giacalone and Jaeger, 2023). Information influence played a pivotal role as well, with message framing affecting consumers' willingness to pay for CM products (Zhang et al., 2022). Social influence, both through peer opinions and social image motivations, shaped consumer attitudes too (Chong et al., 2022; Leong, 2022). Additionally, perceived exclusivity and regulatory considerations influenced consumer attitudes, highlighting the need for a holistic approach.

The relationship between attitudes and intentions played an important role in consumer acceptance. Positive attitudes towards the environmental benefits of cultured meat were associated with a higher intention to accept it (Dean et al., 2023). Positively framed messages influenced attitudes, leading to greater intentions to purchase artificial meat products (Zhang et al., 2022). Creating a sense of exclusivity through scarcity appeals positively affected consumer intentions to try cultured meat (Arango et al., 2023).

The dynamic interplay between internal and external factors in shaping attitudes underscored the complexity of consumer perceptions towards cultured and artificial meat. The overview highlighted the role of attitudes in shaping consumer intentions, emphasising the importance of cultivating positive attitudes to drive the adoption of these innovative food products.

4 The Conceptual Framework – CAPA Model

This section builds upon the exploration of factors affecting consumer behavior and decision-making, obtained from the SLR. It takes a step towards constructing a tailored conceptual framework aimed at assessing consumer responses to innovative food products, with a focus on CM. In acknowledging the limitations of existing work within this context, the development of a more holistic and adaptable conceptual framework becomes imperative, particularly to address the nuanced interplay of decision factors influencing consumer behavior during the pre-purchase stage of CM. This section presents the conceptual framework developed from this research, called CAPA (Cultured Meat Attitude and Perception Assessment).

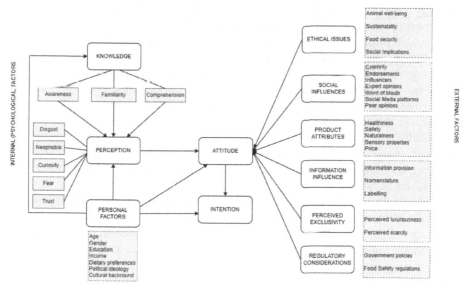

Fig. 2. Cultured Meat Attitude and Perception Assessment (CAPA) framework

Firstly, the CAPA model (Fig. 2) introduces a multidimensional approach to knowledge, encompassing awareness, comprehension, and familiarity, as a foundational element. This dimension recognises that consumers' knowledge about cultured meat goes beyond mere awareness and includes a deeper understanding of the product. It shows the dynamic nature of the knowledge construct, acknowledging that consumers may transition between different levels of knowledge, influencing their perceptions towards

CM. Consequently, the model aims to illustrate the connections between these knowledge dimensions and their impact on consumer perceptions and attitudes towards CM. By examining how awareness, comprehension, and familiarity interact with the perception construct, the framework offers insights into the cognitive processes underlying consumer decision-making about the product. This approach to knowledge about CM acknowledges that informed decisions about cultured meat require more than surface-level awareness (Pakseresht et al., 2022).

Secondly, the proposed model incorporates the construct of perception, including emotional responses such as fear, neophobia, disgust, trust, and curiosity. This addition illustrates the emotional dimension of consumer decision-making, which can strongly influence attitudes and intentions (Bettman and Park, 1980; Verbeke et al., 2015a, 2015b; Hornsey and Fielding, 2017). Within the CAPA framework, perception is showed as an interplay between cognitive (knowledge construct) and affective processes (emotions, feelings, attitude), shaping consumer intentions towards CM. By recognising the varied nature of perception, the CAPA model provides a comprehensive understanding of the factors driving consumer behavior in the context of CM adoption.

Thirdly, the CAPA model places significant emphasis on external factors that can impact consumer attitudes and intentions. These external factors include Ethical Issues (sustainability, animal well-being, food security, social implications), Social Influences (celebrity endorsements, influencers, expert opinions, word-of-mouth, social media platforms, peer opinions), Product Attributes (healthiness, safety, naturalness, sensory properties, price), Information Influence (information provision, nomenclature, labelling), Perceived Exclusivity (perceived luxuriousness, perceived scarcity), Regulatory considerations (government policies, food safety regulations). While existing frameworks, such as Theory of Planned Behaviour (TPB) acknowledges the influence of external factors to some extent (Ajzen, 1991), they may not comprehensively address the dynamics of these influences in the context of CM. By integrating the external influences into the framework, CAPA provides a more complete understanding of the contextual factors shaping consumer attitudes and intentions towards CM, enabling researchers and industry practitioners to develop targeted interventions and strategies to promote the acceptance and adoption of CM products.

While CAPA model shares some commonalities with the existing models in recognising the importance of attitudes and intentions, the proposed framework extends further by incorporating additional dimensions such as knowledge, interest, perception, and a more comprehensive consideration of external influences. These additions allow to provide a more holistic understanding of consumer behavior in the context of emerging food products like cultured meat.

5 Contribution to New Knowledge

Having established the CAPA model as a response to the nuanced dynamics of consumer behaviour, it is important to explore the broader landscape and evaluate existing models that have traditionally shaped the understanding of consumer decision-making. One foundational model for understanding consumer behavior is the Attention, Interest, Desire, Action (AIDA) model (Lavidge and Steiner, 1961), which consists of four stages:

Attention, Interest, Desire, and Action. Commencing with Attention, where consumers become aware, the process unfolds through cultivating Interest, transforming into Desire, and culminating in Action. Another, the Consumer Decision Journey (CDJ) model, provides a comprehensive perspective by dividing the consumer journey into three phases: pre-purchase, purchase, and post-purchase (Lemon and Verhoef, 2016). Understanding the pre-purchase stage is important as it represents the initial phase of the consumer decision journey, where consumers first encounter a product or brand, prompting their Attention. During this stage, consumers accumulate knowledge and develop Interest in the product, simultaneously forming Desire based on the gathered information. The journey then progresses to Action, marking the point where consumers make their ultimate decision. In the context of CM, it is during this phase that consumers become aware of cultured meat, acquire knowledge about it, and initiate the formation of their attitudes (Pakseresht et al., 2022). Several factors, including knowledge, external influences, and emotional responses, come into play during this stage, influencing consumers' eventual decisions (Fishbein, 1963; Lemon and Verhoef, 2016).

Since cultured meat has not yet reached the market, the purchase phase, involving interactions with the product, brand, and overall purchase experience, cannot be assessed and therefore, is not applicable. Similarly, the post-purchase phase, encompassing consumer experiences following product consumption, engagement, and potential word-of-mouth interactions, cannot be observed as there is no tangible product for consumers to evaluate (Lemon and Verhoef, 2016). Nonetheless, the pre-purchase stage serves as an opportunity for investigating consumer attitudes and intentions towards CM. In this context, the research aims to delve into the factors that influence this critical stage of decision-making, specifically focusing on knowledge, perceptions, and external influences.

While the AIDA and CDJ models have proven valuable in traditional contexts, their limitations surface when applied to the exploration of consumer behavior in the context of food innovations like CM. These models predominantly focus on the stages of Attention, Interest, Desire, and Action, potentially overlooking the intricate dynamics of consumer responses to innovative food products (Lavidge and Steiner, 1961). They may not fully accommodate the multifaceted nature of attitudes shaped by factors like knowledge, emotions (fear, disgust, curiosity, neophobia, and skepticism), and external influences, which are particularly pertinent in terms of CM (Hornsey and Fielding, 2017; Verbeke et al., 2015a, 2015b). Moreover, they may only partially emphasise external influences, such as marketing and advertising, potentially falling short in comprehensively addressing the diverse set of external drivers and barriers that significantly affect consumer attitudes and intentions regarding CM. These include perceived exclusivity, ethical considerations, societal influences, product information, product attributes, and regulatory considerations. Finally, these conventional models may provide limited attention to the multidimensional aspect of knowledge (encompassing awareness, comprehension, and familiarity), which plays an important role in influencing consumer behavior and decision-making in the context of cultured meat (Pakseresht et al., 2022). Given these complexities, there is a need for a more holistic and adaptable framework that can better capture the nuanced dynamics in consumer responses to novel food innovations such as CM.

Considering other relevant frameworks for understanding consumer behavior in the pre-purchase stage, where attitudes and intentions play a primary role, the Technology Acceptance Model (TAM) (Davis, 1986) emerges as a well-recognised theory tailored for technology adoption. TAM primarily focuses on the interplay between perceived ease of use and usefulness, significantly influencing users' attitudes and subsequent behavioral intentions towards technology (Davis, 1986). However, its applicability to understanding consumer behavior regarding novel food products like CM may be limited due to its focus on technology acceptance. While TAM offers insights into technology adoption, it may not fully capture the complexities associated with consumer attitudes and behaviors towards CM (Venkatesh et al., 2003). The model's emphasis on technology-related factors, such as perceived ease of use and usefulness, may overlook elements integral to food acceptance, such as sensory perceptions, ethical considerations, cultural norms (Venkatesh et al., 2003). Furthermore, TAM's focus on perceived ease of use and usefulness may not fully account for the emotional and ethical dimensions influencing consumer acceptance of CM, where factors like disgust, curiosity, and ethical concerns play a role (Hornsey and Fielding, 2017; Verbeke et al., 2015a, 2015b). Therefore, while TAM provides valuable insights into technology adoption, its suitability for understanding consumer behavior towards novel food innovations like CM may be limited.

To address these limitations and offer a more comprehensive framework for understanding consumer behaviour in the context of cultured meat, the Theory of Planned Behavior (TPB) appears as a relevant option. Developed as an extension of the Theory of Reasoned Action (TRA), TPB emphasises attitudes, subjective norms, and perceived behavioural control, providing insights into consumer behaviour (Ajzen, 1991). While TPB focuses on these key elements, the proposed CAPA framework extends the scope, encompassing a wider array of factors to offer a deeper understanding in the context of CM. In contrast to TPB's emphasis, CAPA introduces additional dimensions, including emotional responses, external influences, and the multidimensional aspect of knowledge. TPB suggests that attitudes, subjective norms, and perceived behavioral control collectively shape an individual's intentions, guiding their behaviour (Fishbein, 1963; Ajzen, 1985). This aligns with the significance of attitudes driven by knowledge and external influences in shaping consumer perceptions of CM. External factors such as, marketing strategies, societal trends, and regulatory considerations influence consumer attitudes, along with subjective norms reflecting societal expectations (Ajzen and Fishbein, 1980). While TPB acknowledges the importance of these factors, the CAPA framework further enhances understanding by considering additional dimensions. Although TPB centers on attitudes, subjective norms, and perceived behavioural control, CAPA extends beyond these components, offering a more holistic perspective on consumer behavior in the pre-purchase stage.

The evaluation of models, from AIDA and CDJ to TAM and TPB, highlights the importance of a nuanced understanding of the consumer decision-making, particularly in the context of CM. In addressing these complex dynamics, the CAPA model provides to be a useful tool, offering a comprehensive insight into consumer behaviour during the pre-purchase phase.

6 Conclusions

This research discussed the complexities of consumer behaviour concerning cultured meat (CM) acceptance, employing a systematic literature review (SLR) as the primary methodology. The SLR identified and critically evaluated decision factors influencing consumer perceptions and attitudes, serving a foundation for developing the Cultured Meat Attitude and Perception Assessment (CAPA) model. This novel framework extends traditional models like AIDA, CDJ, and TPB, which proved to be limited in capturing the complex dynamics of innovative food products. The developed CAPA model stands as a valuable contribution to understanding consumer behavior in the context of food innovations, providing insights for industry stakeholders, decision-makers, policymakers, and researchers navigating this evolving field.

While this study advances the understanding of consumer behaviour regarding CM acceptance through the design of the CAPA model, it is important to acknowledge limitations in both the overall paper and the proposed framework. Firstly, the generalisability of findings may be restricted by the SLR's scope, which primarily encompasses existing literature rather than incorporating real-world data or diverse demographic perspectives. Secondly, while comprehensive, the CAPA framework itself is subject to certain constraints. For instance, its dependence on self-reported data for understanding consumer attitudes and perceptions may introduce response biases and limitations in accurately capturing the complexities of consumer behaviour. Future research could address these limitations by incorporating diverse methodological approaches, such as empirical studies and qualitative research, to provide a better understanding of consumer behaviour and enhance the generalisability of findings.

Considering the implications of the CAPA framework, it reveals its potential applications beyond CM, including other innovative foods such as 3D printed food products, cultured seafood, cultured eggs, as well as other consumer behaviour contexts, such as the acceptability of healthcare treatments. Additionally, examining the practical implications of applying the CAPA framework for stakeholders such as food manufacturers, marketers, policymakers, and researchers could be beneficial, as insights gained could inform strategic decision-making, product development, and policy initiatives to promote consumer acceptance of novel food technologies.

The next step of this study will be firstly, to conduct a sentiment analysis using data from Twitter to refine the conceptual framework, exploring possible additional factors that may influence consumer perceptions and attitudes towards CM. This will be followed by collecting primary data via a questionnaire survey and analysing the responses through Structural Equation Modelling to quantify the relationships between different constructs and factors within the CAPA model.

Acknowledgments. This research was conducted as part of a Doctoral Training Account (DTA) funded by the University of Plymouth.

References

Ajzen, I.: From intentions to actions: a theory of planned behavior. In: Kuhl, J., Beckmann, J. (eds.) Action Control: From Cognition to Behavior, pp. 11–39. Springer, Heidelberg (1985). https://doi.org/10.1007/978-3-642-69746-3_2

Ajzen, I.: The theory of planned behavior. Organ. Behav. Hum. Decis. Process. **50**(2), 179–211 (1991)

Ajzen, I., Fishbein, M.: Understanding Attitudes and Predicting Social Behavior. Prentice-Hall, Englewood Cliffs (1980)

Arango, L., Chaudhury, S.H., Septianto, F.: The role of demand-based scarcity appeals in promoting cultured meat. Psychol. Mark. **40**(8), 1501–1520 (2023)

Arora, R.S., Brent, D.A., Jaenicke, E.C.: Is India ready for alt-meat? Preferences and willingness to pay for meat alternatives. Sustainability **12**(11), 4377 (2020)

Asioli, D., Bazzani, C., Nayga, R.M., Jr.: Are consumers willing to pay for in-vitro meat? An investigation of naming effects. J. Agric. Econ. **73**(2), 356–375 (2022)

Asioli, D., et al.: 'Consumers' valuation of cultured beef Burger: a multi-country investigation using choice experiments. Food Policy **112** (2022)

Baum, C.M., Bröring, S., Lagerkvist, C.-J.: Information, attitudes, and consumer evaluations of cultivated meat. Food Qual. Prefer. **92** (2021)

Baum, C.M., De Steur, H., Lagerkvist, C.-J.: First impressions and food technology neophobia: examining the role of visual information for consumer evaluations of cultivated meat. Food Qual. Prefer. **110**, 104957 (2023)

Baum, C.M., Verbeke, W., De Steur, H.: Turning your weakness into my strength: how counter-messaging on conventional meat influences acceptance of cultured meat. Food Qual. Prefer. **97**, 104485 (2022)

Bekker, G.A., Fischer, A.R.H., Tobi, H., van Trijp, H.C.M.: Explicit and implicit attitude toward an emerging food technology: the case of cultured meat. Appetite **108**, 245–254 (2017)

Bekker, G.A., Tobi, H., Fischer, A.R.H.: Meet meat: an explorative study on meat and cultured meat as seen by Chinese, Ethiopians and Dutch. Appetite **114**, 82–92 (2017)

Bettman, J.R., Park, C.W.: Effects of prior knowledge and experience and phase of the choice process on consumer decision processes: a protocol analysis. J. Consum. Res. **7**(3), 234–248 (1980)

Booth, A., Papaioannou, D., Sutton, A.: Systematic Approaches to a Successful Literature Review. Sage Publications, Thousans Oaks (2012)

Bryant, C., van Nek, L., Rolland, N.C.M.: European markets for cultured meat: a comparison of Germany and France. Foods **9**(9) (2020)

Bryant, C.J., Anderson, J.E., Asher, K.E., Green, C., Gasteratos, K.: Strategies for overcoming aversion to unnaturalness: the case of clean meat. Meat Sci. **154**, 37–45 (2019)

Bryant, C.J., Barnett, J.C.: What's in a name? Consumer perceptions of in vitro meat under different names. Appetite **137**, 104–113 (2019)

Califano, G., Furno, M., Caracciolo, F.: Beyond one-size-fits-all: consumers react differently to packaging colors and names of cultured meat in Italy. Appetite **182**, 106434 (2023)

Chong, M., Leung, A.K., Lua, V.: A cross-country investigation of social image motivation and acceptance of lab-grown meat in Singapore and the United States. Appetite **173**, 105990 (2022)

Choudhury, D., Tseng, T.W., Swartz, E.: The business of cultured meat. Trends Biotechnol. **38**(6), 573–577 (2020)

Davis, F.D.: A Technology Acceptance Model for Empirically Testing New End-User Information Systems: Theory and Results. Sloan School of Management, Massachusetts Institute of Technology (1986)

Da Silva, C.P., Semprebon, E.: How about cultivated meat? The effect of sustainability appeal, environmental awareness and consumption context on consumers' intention to purchase. J. Food Prod. Mark. **27**(3), 142–156 (2021)

da Silva, M.B.D.O., da Cunha, C.F.: Understanding the perception of potential consumers of cultured meat using free word association. REMark **21**(5), 1527–1573 (2022)

Denyer, D., Tranfield, D.: Producing a systematic review. In: Buchanan, D., Denyer, D.A. (eds.) Handbook of Organizational Research Methods, pp. 671–689. Sage Publications, Thousand Oaks (2009)

de Oliveira, G.A., Domingues, C.H.d.F., Borges, J.A.R.: Analyzing the importance of attributes for Brazilian consumers to replace conventional beef with cultured meat. PLoS ONE **16**(5), e0251432 (2021)

de Oliveira Padilha, L.G., Malek, L., Umberger, W.J.: Consumers' attitudes towards lab-grown meat, conventionally raised meat and plant-based protein alternatives. Food Qual. Prefer. **99**, 104573 (2022)

Dean, D., et al.: Should I really pay a premium for this? Consumer perspectives on cultured muscle, plant-based and fungal-based protein as meat alternatives. J. Int. Food Agribus. Mark. 1–25 (2023)

Dupont, J., Fiebelkorn, F.: Attitudes and acceptance of young people toward the consumption of insects and cultured meat in Germany. Food Qual. Prefer. **85**, 103983 (2020)

Dupont, J., Harms, T., Fiebelkorn, F.: Acceptance of cultured meat in germany-application of an extended theory of planned behaviour. Foods **11**(3) (2022)

Fernandes, A.M., Teixeira, O.d.S., Revillion, J.P., Souza, Â.R.L.d.: Beef as a socio-cultural identity: rural and urban consumers' attitudes from Rio Grande do sul, Brazil, facing cultured beef. J. Rural Stud. **95**, 438–448 (2022)

Fernandes, A.M., Teixeira, O.d.S., Fantinel, A.L., Revillion, J.P.P., Souza, Â.R.L.d.: Technological prospecting: the case of cultured meat. Future Foods **6**, 100156 (2022)

Fishbein, M.: An investigation of the relationships between beliefs about an object and the attitude toward that object. Hum. Relat. **16**(3), 233–239 (1963)

Giacalone, D., Jaeger, S.R.: Consumer acceptance of novel sustainable food technologies: a multi-country survey. J. Clean. Prod. **408** (2023)

Gómez-Luciano, C.A., de Aguiar, L.K., Vriesekoop, F., Urbano, B.: Consumers' willingness to purchase three alternatives to meat proteins in the United Kingdom, Spain, Brazil and the Dominican Republic. Food Qual. Pref. **78** (2019)

Gousset, C., et al.: Perception of cultured "meat" by French consumers according to their diet. Livest. Sci. **260**, 104909 (2022)

Hamlin, R.P., McNeill, L.S., Sim, J.: Food neophobia, food choice and the details of cultured meat acceptance. Meat Sci. **194**, 108964 (2022)

Hocquette, É., Liu, J., Ellies-Oury, M.-P., Chriki, S., Hocquette, J.-F.: Does the future of meat in France depend on cultured muscle cells? Answers from different consumer segments. Meat Sci. **188**, 108776 (2022)

Hornsey, M.J., Fielding, K.S.: Attitude roots and jiu jitsu persuasion: understanding and overcoming the motivated rejection of science. Am. Psychol. **72**(5), 459–473 (2017)

Hubalek, S., Post, M.J., Moutsatsou, P.: Towards resource-efficient and cost-efficient cultured meat. Curr. Opin. Food Sci. **47**, 100885 (2022)

Hwang, J., You, J., Moon, J., Jeong, J.: Factors affecting consumers' alternative meats buying intentions: plant-based meat alternative and cultured meat. Sustainability **12**(14) (2020)

Krings, V.C., Dhont, K., Hodson, G.: Food technology neophobia as a psychological barrier to clean meat acceptance. Food Qual. Prefer. **96**, 104409 (2022)

Lavidge, R.J., Steiner, G.A.: A model for predictive measurements of advertising effectiveness. J. Mark. **25**(6), 59 (1961)

Lemon, K.N., Verhoef, P.C.: Understanding customer experience throughout the customer journey. J. Mark. **80**(6), 69–96 (2016)

Leong, A.D.: Framing in the social media era: socio-psychological mechanisms underlying online public opinion of cultured meat. New Media Soc. 1–19 (2022)

Leung, A.K., Chong, M., Fernandez, T.M., Ng, S.T.: Higher well-being individuals are more receptive to cultivated meat: an investigation of their reasoning for consuming cultivated meat. Appetite **184**, 106496 (2023)

Li, H., Van Loo, E.J., van Trijp, H.C.M., Chen, J., Bai, J.: Will cultured meat be served on Chinese tables? A study of consumer attitudes and intentions about cultured meat in China. Meat Sci. **197**, 109081 (2023)

Lin-Hi, N., Reimer, M., Schäfer, K., Böttcher, J.: Consumer acceptance of cultured meat: an empirical analysis of the role of organizational factors. J. Bus. Econ. **93**(4), 707–746 (2023)

Liu, J., Hocquette, E., Ellies-Oury, M.P., Chriki, S., Hocquette, J.F.: Chinese consumers' attitudes and potential acceptance toward artificial meat. Foods **10** 2) (2021)

Mancini, M.C., Antonioli, F.: Exploring consumers' attitude towards cultured meat in Italy. Meat Sci. **150**, 101–110 (2019)

Rodríguez Escobar, M.I., et al.: Analysis of the cultured meat production system in function of its environmental footprint: current status, gaps and recommendations. Foods **10**(12), 2941 (2021)

Motoki, K., Park, J., Spence, C., Velasco, C.: Contextual acceptance of novel and unfamiliar foods: insects, cultured meat, plant-based meat alternatives, and 3D printed foods. Food Qual. Prefer. **96** (2022)

Onwezen, M.C., Bouwman, E.P., Reinders, M.J., Dagevos, H.: A systematic review on consumer acceptance of alternative proteins: pulses, algae, insects, plant-based meat alternatives, and cultured meat. Appetite **159**, 105058 (2021)

Palmieri, N., Perito, M.A., Lupi, C.: Consumer acceptance of cultured meat: some hints from Italy. Br. Food J. **123**(1), 109–123 (2020)

Pakseresht, A., Ahmadi Kaliji, S., Canavari, M.: Review of factors affecting consumer acceptance of cultured meat. Appetite **170**, 105829 (2022)

Piochi, M., Micheloni, M., Torri, L.: Effect of informative claims on the attitude of Italian consumers towards cultured meat and relationship among variables used in an explicit approach. Food Res. Int. **151**, 110881 (2022)

Rosenfeld, D.L., Tomiyama, A.J.: Would you eat a burger made in a petri dish? Why people feel disgusted by cultured meat. J. Environ. Psychol. **80** (2022)

Ruzgys, S., Pickering, G.J.: Perceptions of cultured meat among youth and messaging strategies. Front. Sustain. Food Syst. **4** (2020)

Ryynanen, T., Toivanen, A.: Hocus-pocus tricks and moral progressions: the emerging meanings of cultured meat in online news comments. Food Cult. Soc. **26**(3), 591–620 (2023)

Septianto, F., Quach, S., Thaichon, P., Japutra, A.: Novel products and advertising visuals: the mediating role of perceived luxuriousness on willingness to try clean meat products. Int. J. Advert. **42**(5), 916–944 (2023)

Septianto, F., Sung, B.L.Y., Duong, C., Conroy, D.: Are two reasons better than one? How natural and ethical appeals influence consumer preferences for clean meat. J. Retail. Consum. Serv. **71** (2023)

Shan, L.J., Jiao, X.L., Wu, L.H., Shao, Y.C., Xu, L.L.: Influence of framing effect on consumers' purchase intention of artificial meat-based on empirical analysis of consumers in seven cities. Front. Psychol. **13** (2022)

Siegrist, M., Bearth, A., Hartmann, C.: Food disgust sensitivity influences the perception of food hazards: results from longitudinal and cross-cultural studies. Appetite **153**, 104742 (2020)

Siegrist, M., Hartmann, C.: Perceived naturalness, disgust, trust and food neophobia as predictors of cultured meat acceptance in ten countries. Appetite **155**, 104814 (2020)

Siddiqui, S.A., Khan, S., Ullah Farooqi, M.Q., Singh, P., Fernando, I., Nagdalian, A.: Consumer behavior towards cultured meat: a review since 2014. Appetite **179**, 106314 (2022)

Specht, A.R., Rumble, J.N., Buck, E.B.: "You call that meat?" investigating social media conversations and influencers surrounding cultured meat. J. Appl. Commun. **104**(1) (2020)

Stephens, N., Di Silvo, L., Dunsford, I., Ellis, M., Glencross, A., Sexton, A.: Bringing cultured meat to market: technical, socio-political, and regulatory challenges in cellular agriculture. Trends Food Sci. Technol. **78**, 155–166 (2018)

Tomiyama, A.J., Kawecki, N.S., Rosenfeld, D.L., Jay, J.A., Rajagopal, D., Rowat, A.C.: Bridging the gap between the science of cultured meat and public perceptions. Trends Food Sci. Technol. **104**, 144–152 (2020)

Tsvakirai, C.Z., Nalley, L.L., Makgopa, T.: Development and validation of a cultured meat neophobia scale: industry implications for South Africa. Sci. Afr. **20** (2023)

Venkatesh, V., Morris, M.G., Davis, G.B., Davis, F.D.: User acceptance of information technology: toward a unified view. MIS Q. **27**(3), 425–478 (2003)

Verbeke, W., Hung, Y., Baum, C.M., De Steur, H.: The power of initial perceived barriers versus motives shaping consumers' willingness to eat cultured meat as a substitute for conventional meat. Livest. Sci. **253**, 104705 (2021)

Verbeke, W., et al.: 'Would you eat cultured meat?': Consumers' reactions and attitude formation in Belgium, Portugal and the United Kingdom. Meat Sci. **102**, 49–58 (2015)

Verbeke, W., Sans, P., Van Loo, E.J.: Challenges and prospects for consumer acceptance of cultured meat. J. Integr. Agric. **14**(2), 285–294 (2015)

Weinrich, R., Strack, M., Neugebauer, F.: Consumer acceptance of cultured meat in Germany. Meat Sci. **162**, 107924 (2020)

Wilks, M., Phillips, C.J.: Attitudes to in vitro meat: a survey of potential consumers in the United States. PLoS ONE **12**(2), e0171904 (2017)

Wilks, M., Phillips, C.J.C., Fielding, K., Hornsey, M.J.: Testing potential psychological predictors of attitudes towards cultured meat. Appetite **136**, 137–145 (2019)

Zhang, J., Shi, H., Sheng, J.: The effects of message framing on novel food introduction: evidence from the artificial meat products in China. Food Policy **112**, 102361 (2022)

Zhang, M., Li, L., Bai, J.: Consumer acceptance of cultured meat in urban areas of three cities in China. Food Control **118**, 107390 (2020)

If Digital Tools are the Solution to Knowledge Transfer, What is the Problem?

Pierre-Emmanuel Arduin[1]($\boxtimes$) and Saliha Ziam[2]

[1] Université Paris-Dauphine, PSL, DRM UMR CNRS 7088, Paris, France
pierre-emmanuel.arduin@dauphine.psl.eu
[2] School of Business Administration, Université TÉLUQ, Montreal, Canada
saliha.ziam@teluq.ca

Abstract. This paper investigates the adequacy of using digital tools as a solution for knowledge transfer and especially for tacit knowledge transfer. Based on individual interpretations (sense-reading), tacit knowledge is more difficult to verbalize and transfer with information systems and digital tools. The expansion of such tools leads to a great risk of neglecting this type of knowledge which is, nevertheless, essential to decision-making and action.

In this article, we argue that the transfer of tacit knowledge through digital tools can be improved by understanding their actual tacit knowledge transfer potential and raising awareness on their limits. The efforts to adapt and use digital tools must consider the degree of knowledge tacitness and the role of people as knowledge brokers who facilitate the socialization between stakeholders to ensure common interpretations.

Indeed, digital tools supporting a social dimension significantly and positively affect tacit knowledge transfer when they ensure trust, reciprocity, and shared goals. Knowledge brokers, recognized for their role as intermediaries between different networks, can facilitate exchanges in these new and not so new spaces.

Keywords: Tacit Knowledge · Knowledge Transfer · Knowledge Brokers · Digital Tools · Socialization

1 Introduction

Given the ubiquity, universality and, above all, facility with which digital tools makes it possible to disseminate information, it is very tempting to consider it sufficient for knowledge transfer. Yet, the research on knowledge transfer clearly demonstrates that the choice of knowledge transfer strategies must be made based on the objective being pursued, the nature of the knowledge to be shared, the needs and skills of the target users and the contextual conditions [50]. Indeed, research in this field is seeking to identify the best strategies to inform, promote changes in attitude, influence decision making or improve professional and organizational practices. A wide variety of activities can help to achieve this, such as knowledge dissemination (decision-making tools, policy briefs), knowledge sharing (practice community, knowledge brokering), social influence (opinion leaders, champions), facilitation (mentoring and supervision) or the use of incentives

© The Author(s), under exclusive license to Springer Nature Switzerland AG 2024
S. P. Duarte et al. (Eds.): ICDSST 2024, LNBIP 506, pp. 126–138, 2024.
https://doi.org/10.1007/978-3-031-59376-5_10

and reinforcement (audits and feedback, reminder systems, etc.). Some of these strategies require a high level of user interaction and engagement [10], particularly when seeking change in behavior, innovation scaling or political influence, while others are better adapted to digital knowledge-transfer processes (decision-making tools, reminder systems, etc.).

Digital tools help to improve practices and decision making by enabling access to evidence in a timely manner, while facilitating communication between knowledge producers and target users (practitioners, managers, or decision-makers). These tools have the potential to accelerate knowledge transfer and improve practices and decision making. However, to date, there is little evaluation of the effects of these new learning spaces on the dynamic of actors' exchanges and engagement, as well as their actual effectiveness. It is also worth inquiring as to their congruence with knowledge transfer strategies that require more sustained interactions to transfer tacit knowledge. Existing studies do not allow us to identify the optimal conditions for these spaces to genuinely support knowledge appropriation and its use by actors in the field. And yet, this phase of knowledge integration is crucial for the success of knowledge transfer. We propose then to address the question of the adequacy of using digital tools as a solution to knowledge transfer and particularly tacit knowledge transfer.

In this article, we first introduce background theories on knowledge transfer, knowledge brokering, and tacit knowledge. Second, we propose a reflection on tacit knowledge transfer through digital tools. Third, we discuss knowledge brokering and the importance to consider the degree of knowledge tacitness, as well as the need to evaluate the effectiveness of digital tools to transfer tacit knowledge.

2 Background Theory

2.1 Knowledge Transfer and Knowledge Brokering

Research on knowledge-transfer (KT) has grown rapidly since the early 2000s. This has led to an abundance of terms to describe it: transfer, mobilization, application, sharing, exchange, use, translation, management [24]. Beyond the terminology, this field of research studies all the steps related to the KT process, from generating research-based knowledge to its use, and all of the implementation strategies employed to facilitate appropriation and use. In this article, we use the following definition: a series of planned and structured activities aimed at encouraging the use of research-generated knowledge in decision-making [11, p. 63].

Knowledge brokering refers to activities that occur between knowledge brokers and users [41, p. 139]. These activities include: (1) information management (monitoring information and identifying evidence), (2) translation of knowledge into simple language and formats adapted to users' needs, (3) training and skill development of users to support their knowledge appropriation.

Various theoretical models have been used to explain the different facets of KT, related to specific issues in various fields. In health and education, these models are more centered on mechanisms to bring knowledge producers (researchers) and users (practitioners and decision-makers) closer together. The first models, the pull model, or the expert model, examine "researchers" behavior and how they disseminate the results of their research. This transfer approach is related to the traditional model of knowledge production, called "Mode 1" [12], where knowledge creation and dissemination are primarily determined by the volume of research produced (scientific articles, reports, marketing of the research, etc.). This passive approach to KT was abandoned in favor of more interactive approaches with the push and interactive models, also referred to as "Mode 2" of knowledge production [12]. More centered on the needs of users and the issues they face in their practices, these new models emphasize the importance of the co-construction of knowledge and stakeholder engagement.

Lastly, from the different perspectives on knowledge transfer emerge three inter-related dimensions: the relational dimension (relationships of trust, partnerships, and collaborations among actors), the structural dimension (creation of spaces for exchange and collaboration) and the cognitive dimension (knowledge creation and capacity development). These three dimensions agree on the social and contextual dimension of the knowledge transfer process [18] and on the importance of the role that intermediate actors, or knowledge brokers, can play in dynamizing these spaces of exchange and knowledge mobilization [41].

Often situated at the interfaces of organizations or networks, knowledge brokers can play a critical role in the process of knowledge creation and transfer. Initially seen as simple intermediaries between the worlds of research and industry, these brokers are now considered genuine agents of change whose support role extends far beyond promoting interactions and involves creating fluid channels of communication. In Canada, this strategy was promoted by the Canadian Health Services Research Foundation (CHSRF) to foster the engagement of practitioners and decision-makers in using evidence. For Lomas [22], knowledge brokers make it possible to attract the attention of decision-makers to the possibilities of innovation in health care and services.

In Canada, six National Collaborating Centers for Public Health (NCCPH) were created to facilitate the integration of evidence in the development of programs and public policies that promote health [42]. Other knowledge transfer infrastructures at the provincial level have also been created to strengthen collaboration between universities and health and social services. These services encompass knowledge monitoring, training in knowledge brokering and support for KT initiatives adapted to partners' needs. In the United Kingdom, the National Health Service implemented 13 knowledge transfer infrastructures, called Collaborations for Leadership in Applied Health Research (CLAHRCs) [16].

While knowledge brokering is often associated with collaboration and with creating connections between actors, this function has evolved greatly over time. A systematic review on knowledge brokering, conducted by Bornbaum et al. [4], revealed a dozen potential activities, ranging from evaluating partners' needs, creating opportunities for exchange, developing tools, and facilitating exchanges to developing skills and supporting change. More recent authors emphasize the knowledge broker's animation skills withing groups and community of practice and their ability to create a shared understanding of the potential benefits of research-based knowledge for the audiences concerned [25]. Such a shared understanding relies on interpretation and on tacit knowledge.

2.2 Tacit Knowledge Transfer and Digital Tools

During the late 1970s and the 1980s, research on the vigorous products development in Japanese companies led to the theory of organizational knowledge creation [17]. Nonaka [34] made then the hypothesis that these companies were doing more than just information processing, drawing on the concept of tacit knowing introduced by Polanyi [39, p. 301]: "Both the way we endow own utterance with meaning and our attribution of meaning to the utterances of others are acts of tacit knowing. They represent sense-giving and sense-reading within the structure of tacit knowing.". Tacit knowledge relies on individual interpretation (*sense-reading*) and is difficult to verbalize, whereas explicit knowledge is tacit knowledge that has been made explicit by someone (*sense-giving*), it can be expressed and processed by information systems and digital tools.

Internalization is one of the four knowledge conversion modes introduced by Nonaka & Takeuchi [36]. These processes highlight the difference between tacit and explicit knowledge: (1) Socialization, where individuals sympathize and directly share tacit knowledge, (2) Externalization, where individuals make explicit their tacit knowledge with words, giving a sense to them (sense-giving), (3) Combination, where existing explicit knowledge is combined to create new explicit knowledge, and (4) Internalization, where words are interpreted and explicit knowledge is converted into tacit knowledge by reading a sense in them (sense-reading). Figure 1 illustrates a bridge between the SECI knowledge conversion modes from Nonaka & Takeuchi [36] and the tacit knowing processes from Polanyi [39].

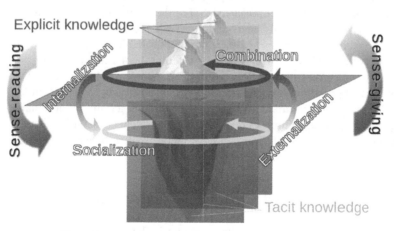

Fig. 1. Knowledge conversion modes and tacit-knowing

The concept of ba focuses on the socialization and can be thought as "a shared space for emerging relationships" [35, p. 40]. It provides a platform of shared spaces for knowledge creation, where one's experiences or reflections on the experiences of others are shared. When separated from ba, knowledge turns into information that can be transmitted through digital tools. Even if information is tangible whereas knowledge is intangible and resides in ba, Nonaka & Konno remarked the possible existence of a cyber ba: "a place of interaction in a virtual world instead of real space and time" [35, p. 47]. Cyber ba represents the Combination mode of the SECI process and allows the combination of explicit knowledge in collaborative environments through digital tools such as on-line networks, group-ware, documentations, and databases.

According to Konno & Schillaci [17], there are two views of knowledge management that Arduin et al. [2], through a study of interactions with information systems and decision aid activities, presented as two complementary approaches: (1) a technological approach focusing on coding explicit, stable, and clearly-defined knowledge, and (2) a managerial and sociotechnical approach focusing on sharing tacit, conjectural, and dynamic knowledge. Such a second approach considers the importance of interpretation to create meaning and how it may induce meaning variance [3].

Authors as Davenport et al. reported some knowledge management projects adopting the technological approach, where "to transfer tacit knowledge from individual into a repository, organizations usually use some sort of community-based electronic discussion" [9, p. 45]. On the contrary, others such as Polanyi clearly insisted on the importance of the managerial and sociotechnical approach to consider individual's tacit knowledge: "the idea of a strictly explicit knowledge is indeed self-contradictory; deprived of their tacit coefficients, all spoken words, all formulae, all maps and graphs, are strictly meaningless" [40, p. 195].

When introducing the concept of community-of-practice, Lave & Wenger [19] argued that learning relies on the participation in communities-of-practice. Such a participation increases gradually but was first peripherally, when individuals were newcomers to the community. Brown & Duguid [5] argued later that supporting formal and informal processes in such communities was needed. For them: "through practice, a community-of-practice develops a shared understanding of what it does, of how to do it, and how it relates to other communities and their practices – in all, a 'world view'." [5, p. 96]. Walsham [46] opened a controversy on such a definition of a community-of-practice: for him, sharing a common purpose does not imply a shared world view. Indeed, communities remain composed of individuals, each holding their own different tacit knowledge. The decision to interact directly face-to-face or through a digital tool remains then an open question. Walsham humbly concluded that this "depends greatly on individual circumstances, but is it likely that a mixture of modes will be better than either extreme" [46, p. 602].

3   A Reflection on Tacit Knowledge Transfer with Digital Tools

As the reader will have noticed, the literature on tacit knowledge mobilized in the previous section has been produced in the late 1990s. In the following, we will present how the literature on tacit knowledge and digital tools, i.e., technology, evolved by focusing first on the possibilities of digital tools to transfer tacit knowledge during the 2000s, second on the specificities of socialization with digital tools to transfer tacit knowledge during the 2010s, and third on capitalizing on the value of employees' tacit knowledge since the 2020s.

3.1   2000–2010: Questioning Digital Tools as a Mean to Transfer Tacit Knowledge

Authors such as Millie Kwan & Balasubramanian [29] pointed out that knowledge repositories often suffer from non-use. These digital tools were supposed to store not only documents with additional content (memos, reports, presentations, etc.), but also discussion databases where participants record their own experiences and can react to others' comments. Actually, an extra burden relied on users to document the repository and there were a lack of structure to mitigate the risk of meaning variance among users. A limit observed was that "much of the [...] discussions in the projects that would have been useful for reference were still carried out on the phone." [29, p. 483].

Taylor [44] proposed a study of Microsoft's NetMeeting, a popular software allowing for voice, video, application-sharing, and text conferencing between two or more parties via TCP/UDP networks [27]. Figure 2.a shows text chat and whiteboard windows, whereas Fig. 2.b shows conversation windows. Marques & Hsu [23] identified the following conferencing features: (1) Application sharing, (2) Shared clipboard, (3) File transfer, (4) Whiteboard, and (5) Chat. According to Taylor (2000), text chat presents an opportunity to develop documentation and application sharing is perceived as extremely useful [44]. Digital tools could then be a way to ensure a common understanding, i.e., tacit knowledge transfer. Johannessen et al. observed that despite of a general optimism concerning these digital tools, these might lead to a "de-emphasizing of tacit knowledge" [15, p. 5]. Indeed, over-emphasizing on explicit knowledge by digital tools investments leads to neglect tacit knowledge and the dialogue between tacit and explicit knowledge occurring during socialization [36].

The enhanced possibility of sharing induced by these digital tools can support tacit knowledge transfer. An individual makes explicit his/her tacit knowledge and shares information through a digital tool (*sense-giving*, according to Polanyi [39]). Another individual receives then such an information through such a digital tool and interprets it to create his/her tacit knowledge (*sense-reading*, according to Polanyi [39]). Nevertheless, as remarked quite early by Nonaka & Takeuchi [36], over-emphasizing digital tools leads to neglect socialization and consequently to neglect tacit knowledge.

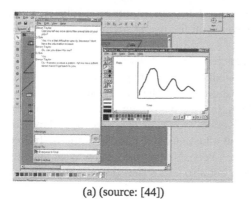
(a) (source: [44])

(b) (source: [31])

Fig. 2. Text chat, whiteboard windows (a), and conversation windows (b) in a video conference

3.2   2010–2020: Focusing on Socialization Through Digital Tools

Young [48] listed in 2010 what he called "Essential KM Methods and Tools to Consider". There are either "Non-IT Methods and Tools" such as brainstorming, storytelling, knowledge café, etc., either "IT Methods and Tools" such as wikis, blogs, expertise locators, etc. (see Fig. 3). In the mid-2010s, Dalkir [8] stated that while "traditional technologies" ensure explicit knowledge transfer, tacit knowledge is more challenging as it is experiential and difficult to articulate into words or documents. She proposed a digital tools selection method relying on Young [48] technologies' list to decide the most appropriate channel to transfer tacit knowledge based on: (1) media richness, i.e., how much multimedia content can be shared, and (2) social presence, i.e. how much people feel they are connecting with other people and not technology. Interestingly, Young [49] proposed in 2020 a revision updating the list of KM tools and techniques ten years after the one proposed in [48].

Liu & Zaraté [20] insisted on the difficulty to transfer tacit knowledge for knowledge based decision support systems, particularly with decision makers from different backgrounds or the existence of confusing terms. Interactive learning environments were then sketched as a way to encourage tacit knowledge transfer across disciplines as well as the use of overlapping teams or joint learning. These authors concluded with a call for further research to develop typologies facilitating more effective transfer of tacit knowledge, notably by including "trust and care, leadership charisma, knowledge culture, concept ba and social network analysis" [20, p. 70].

The advent of social web tools theoretically facilitates tacit knowledge transfer, even if empirical evidences of such a facilitation were lacking in the mid-2010s according to Panahi et al. [38]. Relying on the degree of tacitness [1], Panahi et al. highlighted that tacit knowledge with a low to medium degree of tacitness can be transferred through "appropriate mechanisms" [38]. The degree of knowledge tacitness might also vary from one person to another. For them, digital tools support rich interaction by real-time synchronous communications, even if some social cues are missing such as body language, emotional feelings, eye contact, etc. Chennamaneni & Teng [7] argue that these social cues are more important to transfer knowledge with a high degree of tacitness. Nevertheless, Lopez-Nicolas & Soto-Acosta [21] anticipated quite well that with the advent of high-bandwidth connections, caveats on the use of digital tools to transfer tacit knowledge could disappear.

Media richness as well as social presence, noted by Dalkir [8] as characteristics of appropriate channels to ensure tacit knowledge transfer, are good indicators of what occurred in the 2010-2020s. Technology capabilities were then used as much as possible by individuals to feel connected with others, to reduce meaning variance and to share common understandings. Senders and receivers of tacit knowledge feel as if they were interacting directly, even if digital tools and situations still have limitations. Indeed, Panahi et al. [38] insisted on the importance to consider not only knowledge tacitness that might vary from one person to another, but also social cues that might be missing when interacting through digital tools.

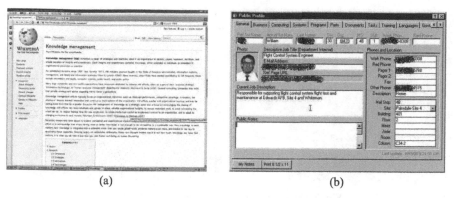

(a)   (b)

Fig. 3. A wiki (a) and an expertise locator (b) (source: [48])

3.3   Since 2020: Capitalizing on the Value of Employees' Tacit Knowledge

Not all digital tools facilitate tacit knowledge transfer. A kind of global awareness about this begins to be found in the literature since the 2020s. Castaneda & Toulson [6] proposed for example a study with 217 participants showing that dialogue-enabling tools such as text messaging and video conferencing systems facilitate tacit knowledge transfer, whereas emails for example did not. For Huie et al. [14], employees must still rely on their colleagues for tacit knowledge.

Introducing digital tools to actually transfer tacit knowledge, Nagle & Adams [32] study the case of pharmaceutical policies and procedures where tacit knowledge is difficult to transfer. They explore the benefits of mixed reality technology to assist knowledge transfer and particularly tacit knowledge. The Microsoft HoloLens2 is presented as a mixed reality technology solution using augmented reality and holographic imagery in a digital headset (Fig. 4). Such an imagery allows the user to understand the end result of an action before s/he performs it, decreasing confusion and meaning variance (see Sect. 2.2). Understanding the power and value of employees' tacit knowledge remain a key step according to Nagle & Adams [32].

Digital tools can do a lot but not everything as explained by Thomas [45]: relying on an empirical research with 497 information technology professionals, he showed that social capital and Web 2.0 significantly affect tacit knowledge transfer. According to him, trust, reciprocity and shared goals contribute to the building of social capital which in turns definitively impacts the transfer of tacit knowledge. Natek & Lesjak [33] proposed a classification of digital tools to support the SECI model, insisting on the importance of socialization to transfer tacit knowledge.

Interestingly, since the 2020s the focus begins to be on cases where tacit knowledge is difficult to transfer. Digital tools can support tacit knowledge transfer but there is a quite global awareness that they sometimes cannot. Understanding the result of an action before performing it via the use of digital tools such as mixed reality technologies can be a way to reduce confusion and meaning variance. Nevertheless, the importance of socialization and direct interaction remains indisputable.

Fig. 4. Mixed Reality Technology (source: [28])

4 Discussion and Recommendations

In this article, we raise the question of the appropriateness of using digital tools for knowledge transfer, particularly for the transfer of tacit knowledge. We believe that the social and relational dimension of knowledge transfer needs to be (re)considered. A growing body of research on knowledge transfer shows that this social dimension can be preserved by people who possess skills adapted to the specificities of knowledge transfer with digital tools. Knowledge brokers whose role of intermediation between different networks is widely recognized can ensure this role as facilitator in these new spaces of exchange. Knowledge brokers are, in fact, more able to animate these places and, above all, to ensure a common understanding of the potential solutions offered by the science for decision-making and the improvement of practices. To do this, they must have the necessary skills to properly manage the dynamics of exchanges and ensure that all stakeholders express their opinions. In addition, knowledge brokers can encourage socialization between stakeholders and thus the dialogue between tacit and explicit knowledge that is necessary for knowledge creation [36].

4.1 The Essential Skills of Knowledge Brokers in Dynamizing Exchange Spaces

Many authors highlight the importance of knowledge brokers' soft skills and their ability to facilitate relational networks by establishing ties of trust and a climate of exchange conducive to the co-construction of knowledge [26]. These facilitating qualities are even more critical today as virtual meetings are becoming the norm. These qualities may appear simple, but in fact require various skills related to online communication, time and people management conducive to information sharing. Knowledge brokers can dynamize spaces for exchange and activate the process of knowledge creation by fostering participants' engagement and motivation in exchanges. They must also help defuse conflicts and ensure that all points of view are expressed.

As pointed out by Meyer, "Knowledge brokers are not simply transmitters of knowledge between communities, they also create new 'negotiated' knowledge based on explicit and tacit knowledge from multiple sources." (translation, cited in [47, p. 431]). While digital tools have made it possible to increase access to knowledge, they do not suffice for mobilizing tacit knowledge. Also, as highlighted in [17], spaces for exchange are also bearers of values and cultural conceptions specific to each community, and the use of technologies does not always have the desired effect. These authors give the example of the use of mobile contact-tracing technologies during the COVID-19 pandemic, which was successful in China but a complete failure in Italy [17, p. 495]. These reflections prompt us to review our conception of what a space for exchange can represent for individuals and to ensure optimal conditions so that these meeting spaces are environments conducive to knowledge transfer.

4.2 The Importance to Consider the Degree of Tacitness and the Need to Evaluate Digital Tools Effectiveness for Tacit Knowledge Transfer

The literature on tacit knowledge and digital socialization tools clearly shows the limits of these tools for transferring tacit knowledge with a high degree of tacitness. Several studies have highlighted the need to preserve the social dimension of knowledge transfer, and the importance of creating spaces for exchange that facilitate listening and the development of relationships [43]. These informal ties develop a sense of trust and belonging to a community, encouraging the transfer of tacit knowledge.

For some authors, the emphasis should be on face-to-face exchanges and a form of mentoring to support the knowledge transfer process [41]. For others, the key is to adapt knowledge transfer strategies and technological tools to the nature of the knowledge and the needs of users [50]. All authors agree that users have to be involved and fully engaged in the whole knowledge transfer process to ensure their appropriation of knowledge. Digital tools such as the social web offers numerous and sophisticated possibilities to optimize the knowledge transfer. However, there are few formal evaluations of its effectiveness for the transfer of knowledge with a high degree of tacitness. It is therefore difficult to conclude on its relevance for knowledge transfer strategies that requires close interactions between stakeholders. Many authors emphasize the importance of additional research to better understand the capabilities of digital tools for knowledge transfer [38, 48].

5 Conclusion and Perspectives

This article stresses the need to re-examine the use of digital tools as a "solution fit for all" type of knowledge transfer. Our findings are consistent with those of other authors on the limitations of these tools for creating optimal conditions for social interactions that support the dialogue between the two types of knowledge: tacit and explicit. This dialogue is the basis of the knowledge creation process as illustrated by the SECI model [36].

Future research should explore new ways to evaluate the effectiveness of these tools and their alignment with the objectives of knowledge transfer, the preferences of individuals, as well as their applicability to different contexts. Extending existing lists such as the one of Natek & Lesjak [33], who proposed a classification of digital tools to support the SECI model, could also be a future research direction, notably through the design of a taxonomy of digital tools supporting tacit knowledge transfer. Also, given the social dimension of knowledge transfer and the need to create optimal conditions for the combination of explicit and tacit knowledge for knowledge creation [36], critical skills for digital knowledge transfer must identified. A skills repository could be developed to better support by knowledge brokers' activities and particularly activities that encourage the transfer of tacit knowledge. Finally, future technological developments must more involve the potential users so that these solutions meet the needs of knowledge transfer process.

References

1. Ambrosini, V., Bowman, C.: Tacit knowledge: some suggestions for operationalization. J. Manag. Stud. **38**(6), 811–829 (2001)
2. Arduin, P.-E., Grundstein, M., Rosenthal-Sabroux, C.: Information and Knowledge System. Wiley, New York (2015)
3. Arduin, P.E.: On the use of cognitive maps to identify meaning variance. In: Joint INFORMS-GDN and EWG-DSS International Conference 2014, Toulouse, France, 10–13 June, pp. 73–80 (2014)
4. Bornbaum, C.C., Kornas, K., Peirson, L., Rosella, L.C.: Exploring the function and effectiveness of knowledge brokers as facilitators of knowledge translation in health-related settings: a systematic review and thematic analysis. Implement. Sci. **10** (2015)
5. Brown, J.S., Duguid, P.: Organizing knowledge. Calif. Manag. Rev. **40**(3), 90–111 (1998)
6. Castaneda, D.I., Toulson, P.: Is it possible to share tacit knowledge using information and communication technology tools? Glob. Knowl. Memory Commun. **70**(8/9), 673–683 (2021)
7. Chennamaneni, A., Teng, J.T.C.: An integrated framework for effective tacit knowledge transfer. In: Proceedings of the Seventeenth Americas Conference on Information Systems (AMCIS 2011), Detroit, MI (2011)
8. Dalkir, K.: The role of technology and social media in tacit knowledge sharing. Int. J. E-Entrepreneurship Innov. (IJEEI) **6**(2), 40–56 (2016)
9. Davenport, T.H., De Long, D.W., Beers, M.C.: Successful knowledge management projects. Sloan Manag. Rev. **39**(2), 43–57 (1998)
10. Flynn, R., et al.: Knowledge translation strategies to support the sustainability of evidence-based interventions in healthcare: a scoping review. Implement. Sci. **18**(1) (2023)
11. Gervais, M.-J., Marion, C., Dagenais, C., François, C., Houlfort, N.: Dealing with the complexity of evaluating knowledge transfer strategies: guiding principles for developing valid instruments. Res. Eval. **25**(1), 62–69 (2016)
12. Gibbons, M., Limoges, C., Nowotny, H., Schwartzman, S., Scott, P., Trow, M.: The New Production of Knowledge: The Dynamics of Science and Research in Contemporary Societies. Sage, London (1994)
13. Grudin, J.: Computer supported cooperative work: history and focus. IEEE Comput. **2**(5), 19–26 (1994)
14. Huie, C.P., Cassaberry, T., Rivera, A.K.: The impact of tacit knowledge sharing on job performance. Int. J. Soc. Educ. Sci. **2**(1), 34–40 (2020)
15. Johannessen, J.A., Olaisen, J., Olsen, B.: Mismanagement of tacit knowledge: the importance of tacit knowledge, the danger of information technology, and what to do about it. Int. J. Inf. Manag. **21**(1), 3–20 (2001)
16. Kislov, R., Wilson, P., Boaden, R.: The 'dark side' of knowledge brokering. J. Health Serv. Res. Policy **22**(2), 107–112 (2017)
17. Konno, N., Schillaci, C.E.: Intellectual capital in society 5.0 by the lens of the knowledge creation theory. J. Intellect. Capital **22**(3), 478–505 (2021)

18. Landry, R., Lamari, M., Amara, N.: The extent and determinants of the utilization of university research in government agencies. Publ. Adm. Rev. **63**(2), 192 (2003)
19. Lave, J., Wenger, E.: Situated Learning: Legitimate Peripheral Participation. Cambridge University Press, Cambridge (1991)
20. Liu, S., Zaraté, P.: Knowledge based decision support systems: a survey on technologies and application domains. In: Joint INFORMS-GDN and EWG-DSS International Conference 2014, Toulouse, France, 10–13 June, pp. 62–72 (2014)
21. Lopez-Nicolas, C., Soto-Acosta, P.: Analyzing ICT adoption and use effects on knowledge creation: an empirical investigation in SMEs. Int. J. Inf. Manag. **30**(6), 521–528 (2010)
22. Lomas, J.: The in-between world of knowledge brokering. BMJ **334**(7585), 129–132 (2007)
23. Marques, O., Hsu, S.: Assessing the feasibility of using Microsoft® NetMeeting TM in distance education. In: International Conference on Engineering and Computer Education (ICECE99), Rio de Janeiro, Brazil (1999)
24. Mckibbon, K.A., et al.: A cross-sectional study of the number and frequency of terms used to refer to knowledge translation in a body of health literature in 2006: a Tower of Babel. Implement. Sci. **5**, 16–26 (2010)
25. McSween-Cadieux, E., Ziam, S., Lane, J.: Les compétences clés en courtage de connaissances. L'importance du soutien à l'implantation et des compétences relationnelles, Revue TUC, Actes de colloque Acfas (2023)
26. Metz, A., Burke, K., Albers, B., Louison, L., Bartley, L.: A practice guide to supporting implementation: what competencies do we need? National Implementation Research Network (2020)
27. Microsoft: Microsoft NetMeeting Protocol, Microsoft Corporation report, 14 July 2016 https://winprotocoldoc.blob.core.windows.net/productionwindowsarchives/MS-MNPR/%5bMS-MNPR%5d-160714.pdf. Accessed 02 Jan 2024
28. Microsoft: Sanofi uses the industrial metaverse to revolutionize training and operational efficiency, Microsoft Corporation report, 15 September 2023. https://customers.microsoft.com/en-us/story/1679230130610461773-sanofi-pharmaceuticals-hololens2. Accessed 02 Jan 2024
29. Millie Kwan, M., Balasubramanian, P.: KnowledgeScope: managing knowledge in context. Decis. Support Syst. **35**(4), 467–486 (2003)
30. Morris, Z.S., Wooding, S., Grant, J.: The answer is 17 years, what is the question: understanding time lags in translational research. J. R. Soc. Med. **104**(12), 510–520 (2011)
31. Mühlenfeld, H.U.: Computergestützte face-to-face interviews über das Internet mit Hilfe von MS NetMeeting. ZA-Information/Zentralarchiv für Empirische Sozialforschung (51), 67–81 (2002)
32. Nagle, D.J., Adams, M.J.: Emerging technologies: empowering people to capture, share and transfer tacit knowledge. Level **3**, 17(2), 4 (2022)
33. Natek, S., Lesjak, D.: Knowledge management systems and tacit knowledge. Int. J. Innov. Learn. **29**(2), 166–180 (2021)
34. Nonaka, I.: Management of Knowledge Creation. Nihon Keizai Shimbun Press, Tokyo (1990)
35. Nonaka, I., Konno, N.: The concept of 'Ba': building a foundation for knowledge creation. Calif. Manag. Rev. Oakland, CA **40**(3), 40–53 (1998)
36. Nonaka, I., Takeuchi, H.: The Knowledge-Creating Company: How Japanese Companies Create the Dynamics of Innovation. Oxford University Press, Oxford (1995)
37. Oliver, K., Innvar, S., Lorenc, T., Woodman, J., Thomas, J.: A systematic review of barriers to and facilitators of the use of evidence by policymakers. BMC Health Serv. Res. **14**, 1–12 (2014)
38. Panahi, S., Watson, J., Partridge, H.: Towards tacit knowledge sharing over social web tools. J. Knowl. Manag. **17**(3), 379–397 (2013)

39. Polanyi, M.: Sense-giving and sense-reading. J. Roy. Inst. Philos. **42**(162), 301–325 (1967)
40. Polanyi, M.: Knowing and Being. Routledge and Kegan Paul, London (1969)
41. Ridde, V., Dagenais, C., Boileau-Falardeau, M.: Une synthèse exploratoire du courtage en connaissance en santé publique. Santé publique **25**(2), 137–145 (2013)
42. Robeson, P.: Networking in public health: exploring the value of networks to the national collaborating centres for public health. National Collaborating Centre for Methods and Tools (2009)
43. Stewart, R., Langer, L., Erasmus, Y.: An integrated model for increasing the use of evidence by decision-makers for improved development. Dev. South. Afr. **36**(5), 616–631 (2019)
44. Taylor, S.J.: Netmeeting: a tool for collaborative simulation modeling. Int. J. Simul. Syst. Sci. Technol. **1**(1–2), 59–68 (2000)
45. Thomas, A.: Promoting IT professionals' tacit knowledge sharing through social capital and web 2.0: the moderating role of absorptive capacity. Kybernetes**52**(12), 5849–5874 (2023)
46. Walsham, G.: Knowledge management: the benefits and limitations of computer systems. Eur. Manag. J. **19**(6), 599–608 (2001)
47. Wye, L., et al.: Collective knowledge brokering: the model and impact of an embedded team. Evidence Policy: J. Res. Debate Pract. **16**(3), 429–452 (2020)
48. Young, R.: Knowledge Management Tools and Techniques Manual. Asian Productivity Organization (2010)
49. Young, R.: Knowledge Management Tools and Techniques Manual. Revised edn. Asian Productivity Organization (2020)
50. Ziam, S., et al.: A scoping review of theories, models and frameworks used or proposed to evaluate knowledge mobilization strategies, Health Res. Policy Syst. **11**(8) (2024)

Author Index

S. P. Duarte et al. (Eds.): ICDSST 2024, LNBIP 506, p. 139, 2024.
https://doi.org/10.1007/978-3-031-59376-5

Printed in the United States
by Baker & Taylor Publisher Services